Other books written by the author:

Marketing Calculator: Measuring and Managing Return on Marketing Investment by Guy R. Powell

ROI of Social Media: How to Improve the Return on Your Social Marketing Investment by Guy R. Powell, Steven Groves, Jerry Dimos

Marketing Machine

The Secret History of the Future of Marketing (ROI)

Guy R. Powell

ISBN: 978-1-4834-8919-3 (sc)
ISBN: 978-1-4834-8921-6 (hc)
ISBN: 978-1-4834-8920-9 (e)

Library of Congress Control Number: 2018908950

Lulu Publishing Services rev. date: 8/28/2018

To my lovely wife and family

Marketing Machine is uniquely global in scope. So many books are US-centric, yet Guy's book incorporates many of the nuances found outside the US. I wish this book were available as we were implementing our ROMI infrastructure. It would have smoothed many of the rough hurdles we had and would have sped up our ability to achieve a higher level of marketing effectiveness.

Petri Huttunen, *Senior Manager, Telia Finland*

Marketing strategy, tactics, analytics and insights all come together with Guy's book. He takes the operational aspects of marketing and combines them with measurement and analysis to show how marketers can deliver predictable revenue. This book will also arm marketing students with the appropriate marketing management tools they will need as they enter the workplace.

Reshma Shah, *Associate Professor of Marketing,*
Emory Goizueta Business School

Marketing Machine provides a road map on how to build a modern marketing organization that is well-positioned for success. Guy has been a great partner helping us implement many of the concepts found in his book and optimize ROMI.

Matthew Quale, *CMO, Brighthouse Financial, Inc.*

This is Guy's fourth and best book on marketing – it really opens and unlocks the Marketing Machine. His work has helped me find high ROI marketing strategies that really work in a digital age and his tools are practical. Finally, the question of what drives high ROI in a marketing. I wish that Guy's Marketing Machine can help marketers all over the world as it has helped me.

Aseem Puri, *Marketing Director, Unilever International*

Guy has created a simple, but elegant roadmap that links the corporate vision to in-market performance by leveraging the power of analytics. This book will enable you to create a "magical" thread to consistently link all marketing activities to in-market performance…read the book once and keep it nearby as a handy "how to" guide.

Garth Viegas, *Global Insights Director, Tata Global Beverages*

Guy's new book provides great approaches to providing confidence in making marketing decisions in both simple and complex marketing environments. It's clear that his recommendations are based on real-life experience in B2B, B2C and B2B2C markets. We look to implement a number of the concepts in Marketing Machine and expect that they will contribute enormously.

Tim Hernquist, *Associate Director, Marketing and Training, Carrier Corporation, Ductless & VRF*

I've worked with Guy on many projects over the years, so I'm always happy when he publishes another book offering his wisdom to the broader market. 'The Marketing Machine' is a very insightful addition to his considerable portfolio. I promise you'll head back to it regularly as a reference. Enjoy!

Nick Popielski, *Vice President, Organic Growth, Spire, Inc.*

Contents

Section One:
Marketing Needs to Be a Machine

Section Three:
Marketing Owns the Future

Acknowledgements

As with any major work there are a lot of people that helped directly and indirectly with the completion of the book. The individuals mentioned below are those that provided direct input. There are many others that provided very keen insights at various stages unrelated to the actual writing but nevertheless influenced the content and theoretical framework.

To begin with I wanted to thank quite a few people that provided real life insights into the structure of many of the key concepts. Many of them we've worked very closely with to build specific thoughts and methods, and directly applied to their businesses. Many provided specific examples and case studies in the book. Others we used to build out and refine specific thoughts. Here I would like to thank Peter Dreyer, Matt Quale, Chia Hsun Chang, Abbie Ding from Brighthouse Financial, Inc., Gail Gallupo and Joe Burns from Aflac Inc., William Peeples, Marcie Shields of Atlanta Gas Light Company, Nick Popielski, now with Spire Energy, formerly with Atlanta Gas Light Company and United Guaranty, and Donna Peeples formerly with Atlanta Gas Light, Steven Stewart, Robert Kirkwood and Susan Hon with Invista, Garth Viegas now with Tata Global Beverages, formerly with MasterCard, and Petri Huttunen with Telia Company.

The more I've gotten into the art and science of marketing effectiveness, the more I've come to depend on a handful of people from around the world that have contributed to the ideas and methodologies found in *Marketing Machine*. I would like to thank Michiel Van De Wattering of Accountable Marketing, Jacques Koster formerly of Op'maat Media, Reshma Shah, Assistant Professor in the Practice of Marketing Emory University and Sophie King with ChinaInno, Rahul Colaco, President FrieslandCampina, Shanghai, Tommaso Pronunzio with Ales Research, Alexander Arbouw with Alpro.

I also interviewed the following persons each of which gave great advice and input into validating and expanding concepts. I would like to thank Bert Thornton formerly of Waffle House, Sam Bernstein formerly with Dollar Express, Rohan Paul at Deloitte Services, Jim Perello of Jeld-Wen, Aseem Puri of Unilever and Paul Johan of Ballast Point Ventures.

Lastly, writing this book, I would especially like to thank my partners with ProRelevant, Ramesh Sundararajan, Andy Cohen, Pulak Ghosh and Steven Groves; and my editors, Laura Paquette, Barbara Tapp, Daniel McMurtry that have provided editing for the book as it progressed. They helped in many ways to significantly enhance the quality and organization of much of the content.

Chapter 1

Introduction

Wouldn't it be great if we could manage a marketing program knowing that each time we put more money in, we would be able to know exactly how much more money we would be able to get out? We know that when we turn on a light we pay for the electricity and we get light. When we put gas into a furnace we get heat. The more gas we put in, the hotter it gets. The more we press on the accelerator, the faster the car goes. In each of these cases there is a near-linear relationship between the fuel and the result. That's what business executives want from their marketing and what shareholders want from their investment. They want to know that if they put in $1,000 or $1,000,000 or $10,000,000, they will be guaranteed to get some positive, known, and repeatable result—a result that is both measurable and closely linked to the level of investment made.

This direct relationship between marketing investment and outcomes is starting to become a reality in the digital space, but only very recently. When we invest in online advertising, we see the number of visits to our website go up; if the website is designed properly and the business model allows it, those clicks turn into conversions and revenue. For many companies, this relationship has been reflected in the past in the hiring of new salespersons, implementing an outbound call center, or investing in direct response TV. Lori Greiner was able to develop great new products and successfully deliver them to market through the popular QVC TV shopping channel.[1] AT&T used 800-numbers and sophisticated call centers to grow their long-distance business.

Many online businesses operate through direct marketing techniques. They were designed from the start to run off purchased exposure which is

---

[1] http://www.lorigreiner.com/meet-lori.html, October 2016

then converted into cash at the checkout. These startups invested all they could into marketing so they could continue to feed their voracious appetites for growth. Zappos[2] was able to get past the challenges of online shoe purchases by removing the risk of the purchase. With a simple and easy returns policy, it didn't matter if the shoe didn't fit or the color wasn't what was expected. The shoes could simply be sent back, with no questions asked.

Marketing needs to be a machine.

Unfortunately, there are many businesses that don't or can't operate that way. They want to be able to put money into marketing on the one side of the machine and see revenue pour out on the other but haven't figured out the formula. They often face these challenges:

- Their brand is unknown and not yet trusted.
- Their consumer purchase cycle is complex and long lasting. It may last 6 months to a year or even longer
- The products and services simply don't lend themselves to being purchased online or in a fast way.
- Sales are shrinking.
- CEOs think that if marketing is more effective, they can squeeze more profit out of the business, by achieving the corporate sales target and spend less on marketing.

Still, the business imperative exists to generate more revenue in a direct response to more marketing investment. This leads to several strategic business questions as to how stakeholders can configure and manage a business so that it can deliver immediate, measurable sales revenue from any marketing investment. The answers to these questions bring an understanding of marketing fundamentals in terms of how messages inserted into the marketplace can influence consumer purchase behavior; in other words, converting a need for some solution into a purchase of your product.

This book will touch on these core issues so that executives can reconfigure not only their business models, but also their marketing models,

---

[2] http://www.zappos.com/c/about-zappos, October 2016

allowing them to simply turn up the marketing volume to deliver more sales *volume* when they need it and in a quantity they can afford. If the business stakeholders are able to understand this connection, they will do what is needed to optimize the level of sales revenue against their operational capacity. And in so doing, they will meet or exceed the returns expected by the owners and shareholders of the company.

There are only a few existing businesses where this clean connection between marketing investment and sales revenue currently exists. Too many things get in the way. Government regulation, competitive action, changes in consumer purchase behavior, and many other factors impede this simple connection. Nevertheless, what businesses require is the ability to build marketing processes based on a relatively accurate model that can consider all of these influences on sales volumes and be able to react so that the quality and quantity of marketing investments can be quickly adjusted to compensate for market changes. In this way, the company can be reasonably assured that they will satisfy their investors with the overall financial returns expected from the business, regardless of the risks in the marketplace. *Marketing needs the agility to be able to quickly move to the right or the left, the top or the bottom, to keep the business on track.*

Marketing needs to be agile.

Many businesses see the challenges facing them but don't react appropriately. Instead of changing the way they do business to respond to the vicissitudes in the marketplace, they continue to trust their tried-and-(un-)true methods. They are too slow to respond to what initially appears to be small market changes, when in reality these small changes are just the early warning signs of looming calamity. Or they wait for one of their competitors or a new entrant to disrupt their business. Or worse yet, they try and cut their way to growth.

Making or responding to disruptive changes is never easy. Sometimes complacent business managers just don't have the fire in the belly to make the changes, or the signs aren't easy to foresee. When the signs are extreme, many managers want to hold on to false beliefs as long as they can because they're afraid of change.

With technological developments coming at us almost daily, in today's market the only thing we know for certain is that constant change is no longer the status quo. *Accelerating* change is the new status quo.

Marketing needs to help the CEO recognize and identify small and large disruptions in the market so that the company can respond and stay on target. Marketing needs to have the agility to fend off a competitive thrust or beat back a new entrant. They need to keep their prices high and drive the brand so that, even in the face of competitive change, they can maintain their margins. In the face of government intrusion creeping into more and more markets, businesses need to be able to respond quickly and correctly to achieve the numbers and deliver profit. And profit, of course, is the *raison d'être* for business.

Depending on the business, the marketing function can be defined incorrectly as, for example, the simple execution of the desires of the sales team. This is common in small B2B organizations. Or, the marketing department can be correctly defined as the builders of the brand and drivers of revenue, which is generally the viewpoint for large consumer companies. Regardless of how it is defined today, the real marketing function encompasses not just the development of brochures, but the definition of the entire consumer experience: how a consumer sees the brand through various media channels, how the consumer experiences the purchase process, how the consumer experiences the product or service, and how that consumer can advocate for the brand after consumption. In some cases, the experience even includes how the product (and its packaging) is disposed of after its usefulness has been depleted (see call-out box: Post-Use Consumer Marketing).

Post-Use Consumer Marketing

Due to strict regulations in many European countries, retail stores are responsible for the collection and recycling of product packaging. Many companies offer free print cartridge recycling. These consumer events are often undervalued: They not only appeal to the eco-conscious consumer, but also provide a new touchpoint for the consumer to experience the brand. In this way, even after the consumer has made their purchase decision the marketer can build up brand value for the next purchase and for possible ongoing social advocacy.

With small and large disruptions taking place more frequently, marketers need to build their ability to learn not just from the past but from the future. They need to constantly monitor the future and be able to adjust their plans to account for upcoming disruptions. They need to combine their short-term view of the future, e.g., the next 90 days, with the long-term expectations of change.

Keeping your ear to the railroad tracks can let you know if a train is coming around the bend. By keeping eyes and ears open through market research, the distribution channel, and tracking external factors such as impending regulation or new competitive entrants, *marketers can make certain they have the information necessary to be prepared for the future looming around the corner or off in the distance.*

Marketing needs to be prepared for the future.

Being prepared for the future also means being able to understand the impact of an impending disruptive event. What will the new entrant do to our pricing or our volumes? What will the shift from brick-and-mortar retail to online do to our long-term position in the market? What will new financial regulations mean to our cost structure and how will we be able to keep our volumes if we need to raise our prices?

How should we best respond? Can we simply lower prices, or offer a Buy-One-Get-One (BOGO)? Or, do we need to respond differently to a new low-priced entrant? Can we beat the competition in building attractive online stores without wreaking havoc on our relationships with our current retailers? Can we support a price increase with more advertising to keep our customers while growing our profit margins?

Marketers need to be able to simulate each of these future scenarios, so they can determine the best response for the expected disruptions. And they need to understand the sensitivity and risk to their response in case the disruptions come faster or are more intense than anticipated. They need to be armed with the right tools to learn from the future. Their simulations and projections must be accurate enough that the rest of the company can have confidence in them—then the company will respond with investment dollars if and when it is necessary to do so.

As opposed to the finance organization, which puts together reports on how well the organization executed in the past, marketing helps the organization to budget for the future, or makes cash available to support the business; as opposed to manufacturing, which builds products to satisfy the now and builds inventory for the potential future, *marketing must own the future.*

Marketing must own the future.

Marketing needs to make certain that their projections are based on fact so that manufacturing will be prepared with the right level of inventory—too little inventory and demand goes unsatisfied, too much inventory can lead to some future return, write-off, or price-off.

This book, *Marketing Machine,* will explore these four critical topics that help businesses to become best in class and stay best in class.

- Marketing needs to be a machine.
- Marketing needs to be agile.
- Marketing needs to be prepared for the future.
- Marketing must own the future.

Marketing Machine will provide concrete examples of how businesses can implement these four critical dimensions of marketing success. It will provide case studies and also look at the pitfalls hindering execution. It will provide concrete steps as to how CEOs and marketers can transform their marketing processes to sleep and breathe agility.

Justification for the marketing machine

Could you imagine the CEO walking into the CFO's office and asking, "How much cash is in the bank right now?" and getting an answer like, "I really like the color of the bank statements." If the CFO doesn't know the amount of cash in the bank down to the dollar and penny, pound and pence, the CFO should be fired. For this simple yet critical question, the company spends a lot of money in bank service charges and reconciliation and accounting systems to make certain that the company knows exactly how much money is any account at any given moment. When the CFO closes the books out for the month, the numbers are reconciled to exacting standards.

Auditors follow up and make certain that the numbers have been properly calculated and that the right financial accounting standards are followed. The accounting department operates as a machine in closing the books by some fixed date after the close of the month.

Similarly, the VP of Manufacturing spends a lot of money to determine and track the level and number of defects in the manufacturing process. The VP of Customer Service spends money to determine and track the customer service levels in their call centers. Marketing must do the same.

What's important is that each of the major departments in the company spend money, effort, and management time to track, measure and improve their operations. They strive to operate as a machine and work to improve their processes in order to lower costs and/or improve customer satisfaction. In all cases, there are people, processes, and technology in place to operate the corporate functions in an orderly, regular, and predictable way, like a machine.

Marketing needs to do the same. Marketing needs to develop people, processes, and technology so that the company can rely on its impact—only then can it be accountable and predictable with low risk and low cost, but more importantly, high value. The marketing function needs to be transformed to reliably deliver the most revenue for the least cost and least risk possible.

Marketing Accountability Defined

"Marketing accountability refers to the use of metrics to link a firm's marketing actions to financially relevant outcomes and growth over time. This accountability allows marketing to take responsibility for the profit or loss from investments in marketing activities, and to demonstrate the financial contributions of specific marketing programs to the overall financial objectives of the firm, including brand asset value. Return on marketing investment (ROMI), customer acquisition costs, and retention rates are common marketing accountability metrics."

Note: This definition was developed and provided by The Board of Directors of MASB, the Marketing Accountability Standards Board, and now appears in the Common Language Marketing Dictionary.

Chapter 2

Marketing Is Broken

There are many different perceptions of marketing in different companies. For David Hewlett, co-founder of Hewlett Packard, "marketing is too important to be left to the marketing department."[3]

The problems in marketing are manifold. Here are a few of the things that we've seen from our work:

- Rigid planning processes
- Inflexible marketing approaches
- Marketers not trained or unwilling to take risks
- Marketing not tied to achievement, but instead tied to task accomplishment
- Marketers with an aversion to and fear of marketing measurement
- Backwards budgeting
- Agencies in need of a new model for compensation
- Organizational and informational silos
- Marketing that is only external facing
- Marketing that does not benchmark against the best—in and outside of their industries
- Marketing planning that is out of phase with the customer buying cycle
- Marketers who do not plan top down and bottom up

> "In preparing for battle, I have always found that plans are useless but planning is indispensable."
>
> Dwight D. Eisenhower

---

[3] https://www.entrepreneur.com/article/229822, October 2016

Marketing planning process[4]

Planning is critical to the successful functioning of any business, and most marketers are very good at making marketing plans. Almost all marketers at least plan on an annual cycle in line with the annual corporate planning cycle. They put together thoughts for their new actions for the year into a comprehensive action plan outlining how they are going to spend the marketing budget, but not how they are going to achieve the corporate revenue plan. The annual marketing plan includes their spending plans, their creative plans, and their personnel plans. It is often referred to as a strategic marketing plan, but technically, it's only an annual marketing plan.

The annual marketing plan is the foundation against which the marketing team will execute. It should roll up into the corporate strategic plan, which in turn rolls up into the corporate vision. On the other hand, the annual plan is made up of a number of smaller tactical campaigns that are executed throughout the year.

Whereas the strategic plan looks out at the business's strengths and weaknesses, and opportunities and threats to the corporate vision, the annual marketing plan outlines concrete steps to execute against a budget. Marketing plans fail because they simply look to spend against a budget, whereas in fact the annual marketing plan should execute activities to achieve the corporate revenue plan. For many marketers, the annual plan is fixed throughout the year and only gets modified when the company needs to cut back on expenses. Rarely does it connect back to corporate achievement, where it is updated based on success and clearly linked to the level of revenue attributed to it. As shown in Figure 1: Marketing Planning Hierarchy, there is a fuzzy or no connection between marketing planning and corporate achievement, when there should be a firm and clear link between marketing tactics and achievement.

---

[4] https://en.wikiquote.org/wiki/Dwight_D._Eisenhower, October 2016

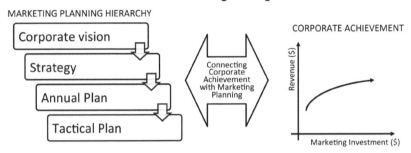

Figure 1: Marketing Planning Hierarchy

The marketing planning process must link directly to corporate success, that is, revenue and profit. In order for marketing to deliver on corporate success, it must link the corporate vision to the strategic plan, to the annual plan, to a rolling planning process updated on a daily, weekly, or monthly basis, based on marketing's ability to support corporate revenue achievement. There needs to be a seamless integration between these planning horizons so that the marketer can make critical day-to-day, week-to-week, and month-to-month adjustments to achieve the numbers. These are the numbers that keep the company alive, that get reported to Wall Street, the financial community, and the shareholders, and that justify further investment in the company. This is why marketers always need to strive to achieve corporate financial objectives. They need to adjust their actions based on opportunities that present themselves and respond to new threats from the competition or other channel or external factors. They must make their annual plans such that the tactics are modifiable based on events unfolding in the marketplace with the goal that these modifications will lead to 100% achievement of the corporate revenue and profit plan.

Inflexible approach

Many marketers are very inflexible in their approach to the market. They are often unwilling to adjust to new realities in the marketplace, or haven't been given the freedom to adjust. Many times, they don't have the experience to know when and where to react. They have moved up through the ranks without formal marketing training. Or worse yet, especially in small business, they've moved from other departments and have landed in marketing

11

because they can execute tasks well. They are task-based as opposed to objectives-based. Their focus is on completing the task and spending the budget so they can get more budget the next year. Their objectives are out of alignment with the company goals, which are to achieve the revenue and profit objectives negotiated and agreed on with the shareholders.

Risk aversion

Marketers are generally risk-averse. Their mortgage isn't on the line, so they can easily put off to next quarter or next year the trial of some new marketing channel or product partnership. Before they make a trial in some new area, they want to see that someone else has had success. Riding on the coattails of the innovative marketer, risk-averse marketers waited many years before they started to invest in online marketing. Others didn't invest very quickly in social media and missed out on many of the early opportunities there. Now the Internet of Things (IoT) is upon us, and those marketers that move first will have an opportunity to disrupt the industry by how they reach their markets through these exciting new opportunities. Those that move last will not reap the rewards of investing early in this new media, distribution, and product channel.

For the CEO

Internet of Things (IoT) – Everything will or can be connected to the Internet. As this happens, many new applications, business opportunities, and profit streams will be developed. New distribution channels will emerge. With everything connected to the Internet, data volumes will explode. Proprietary analytics using this IoT data will become a competitive weapon.

Task accomplishment versus objectives achievement

Task accomplishment thinking is found in many marketing departments that are incentivized based on executing projects on time and under budget, instead of on whether they achieve some objective that is valuable to the company. Some marketing departments with good intentions have begun developing and operating against meaningful KPIs, but without strong leadership discipline these quickly degenerate into simple delivery, as opposed to delivery with the required quality and outcome.

For example, for many small B2B companies, marketing is tasked with the delivery of a certain quantity of leads. This can easily be accomplished by generating a large quantity of leads of any quality, as opposed to the right quantity of leads of a high quality. Marketing thus generates thousands of very cold, invaluable leads instead of a few high-quality leads. Lead quality is critical to success and is often the major point of friction between the marketing team and the sales team for B2B companies.

This occurs because marketing incentives aren't properly aligned. The sales team's commissions (and their mortgages) are dependent on the quality of the lead. The marketing bonus and vacation is often only slightly dependent on the lead quality. If marketing gets lucky they can take the family on a nice vacation. If the sales team is unlucky, they sell the house and move into an apartment and start working somewhere else.

Marketing measurement and accountability

Marketers have always been measurement-averse. They don't want to be measured on their success, except when it's positive. Many times, answers to questions about the success of a new campaign are "everyone really likes it" as opposed to "it's generating a 14% lift over last year." "It won a creative award," as opposed to "it increased profits by 17%."

Marketers must learn to measure not just everything but the right things. They need to measure their inputs, the right interim metrics or KPIs with the right qualifiers, and then be able to tie each of these metrics to financial success. Marketers need critical dashboards that allow them to project results based on their current KPI achievement—and then they need the flexibility to adjust their plans to make certain they deliver. When the sales team is falling short of achievement goals, they knuckle down and start making cold calls. When the marketing team isn't making the numbers, they go home and hope they do better next quarter. But "Hope is not a strategy." Unfortunately, for most businesses, the next quarter is too late. The stock price plummets, budgets get cut, and the death spiral begins.

For the CEO
Does marketing belong to sales or does sales belong to marketing?

We define marketing as the management of the 4Ps to deliver as much sales at least cost and least risk as fast as possible. The 4Ps include the delivery of messages (the "Promotion" P). Just as messages are delivered to various consumers through various media channels, the sales team is a message delivery channel that has some advantages over others. It is very reactive and can deliver very complex messages in a relatively concise fashion. It is mostly a very expensive channel, but it's major difference to other media channels is that it can take the order. In contrast, orders can't be taken from TV or a print advertisement. In that light, as a message delivery channel, sales must be considered as a comparable channel to others in the media mix. With that in mind, sales should belong to marketing and not the other way around.

Marketing budgeting is backwards.

Since the future is uncertain, marketing needs to be able to react to the vicissitudes in the marketplace; but they also need the resources to be able to respond. Best-in-class businesses are now allocating marketing reserves so that the marketing team is empowered to exceed their short-term spending authority in order to make certain that they are able to deliver the right interim metrics with the right quality so that the company can make the numbers. This flexibility is critical for businesses to avoid the pitfalls of lack of achievement due to marketing missteps.

The marketing reserve is just as important as reserves for bad debt in accounts receivables. Financial accounting principles allow the finance department to accrue a certain level of bad debt expectation. Marketers need the same flexibility to be able to exceed the budgeted spending authority when achievement is low or if a new opportunity with proven ROI presents itself.

Advertising agencies need a new model for compensation.

Many marketers are moving to a partial, performance-based compensation model but not giving their agency the tools and information to make the best decisions for them. They are receiving feedback as to creative quality, but not the complete feedback that would allow them to always make the best decisions. Because the models have been slow in building and are never delivered near live, the feedback as to the most effective media mix is too little too late. Agencies need to be part of the full cycle of execution, measurement, analysis, feedback, and improvement. Only then can the agency deliver on their promise of effective development and execution of media communications in the market. A proper compensation model needs to be determined, free from any media channel rebates and other biases that may distort the performance-based model. The agency must be directly compensated based on successful achievement of the corporate revenue plan, as well as lucrative bonuses for over-achievement.

Organizational and informational silos

Every organization works to break down silos. Only in a few rare cases are siloes warranted. Unfortunately, for most companies, when one gets broken down, two others form. Siloes, however, need to be broken down, especially when it comes to critical information related to making better marketing decisions about owning the future. When critical personal information from the consumer is in a position to be compromised, then there needs to be a wall around it. The only time walls need to be in place is when there is some value, like protection of personal consumer information, or because of adherence to some government regulation. Otherwise, the company needs to work to break down these information and data barriers. The free flow of information to the right person in the decision chain needs to be the over-riding factor when building out the organization, the responsibilities, and the flow of information.

Case Study: Cheese that goes Ka-ching

A few best-in-class companies have truly embraced forward thinking in their marketing operations and have implemented tools to take advantage of the critical value of marketing owning the future. Westland Cheese Group, BV is one of them. Based in the Netherlands, Westland is a globally recognized cheese producer. Their flagship brand, Old Amsterdam, is unsurpassed in its quality and taste, with little change throughout the years.

Case Study: Cheese that goes Ka-ching (cont'd)

Every year the company develops their annual plan for their fiscal year beginning in January. In the Netherlands prior to 2007 the company advertised twice per year, once in the Spring and once in the Fall. As much as they would like to advertise throughout the year, the market is simply not large enough to support enough incremental revenue for continuous advertising. Given their current sales levels and their need to break-through above the clutter, they've found that campaigns lasting about 12 to 16 weeks, twice per year, are very effective. This allows the brand to remind the consumer that for special occasions, Old Amsterdam is just right.

As with each new annual planning cycle, the company engages their advertising agency to develop a new creative concept to be run throughout the year. From 2007 to 2013 they implemented a true marketing machine, where they were able to monitor and react to the current and future success of the campaign. In 2007, they executed the campaign and found that sales didn't increase as per their expectations. Because they were monitoring brand imagery perceptions (awareness, purchase intent, and imagery) on a weekly basis, the brand team was able to quickly deduce that the creative concept was mediocre. Things got worse and in the third week response diminished much faster than planned. At this point the company had three options.

1. The first option was to react immediately: to pull the ad and suffer lackluster sales for the rest of the year. This would have saved money on unused and recoverable advertising expenses, but the sales revenue would never have achieved their target. Not only would this impact their own sales, but their distribution channel would have also suffered lackluster sales.
2. The second option was to continue running the ad and with certainty continue to perform well under plan in the marketplace. This would have been the case had they not been evaluating brand response on a weekly basis.
3. The third option was to pull the new creative and replace it with the creative from the previous year.

Westland chose option three. They were able to quickly switch out the creative executions. The campaign immediately started achieving the expected lift in sales for the remaining weeks of the Spring campaign and subsequently for the full length of the Fall campaign.

In addition, because the company had a strong marketing machine in place they were able to monitor the other activation elements of their campaign to drive significantly more volume through these as well. Due to these new insights, the agility of their market-ing machine, and the ability to look into the future, the company had the confidence to add a third campaign in the following year. With the tracking results from the prior year they had confidence in the expected response of the third campaign to deliver a positive ROI for all three campaign periods. They were able to get back on track and were able to exceed revenue growth expectations over the next 5 years of their strategic plan.

> **Case Study: Cheese that goes Ka-ching (cont'd)**
>
> Once the insights from this initial decision were fully incorporated into their market-ing processes, they were able to review achievement on a weekly basis and were able to recover the early lost sales due to the weak campaign creative and increase them for the rest of the year. Because they were able to see into the future and because of the agility provided by their marketing machine the negative impact of the failed creative execution was mitigated. In addition, the insights garnered helped them beat their current year sales and their 5-year strategic sales plan.*
>
> Note: Case Study courtesy of Westland BV and Jacques Koster, Opmaat Media

Benchmark against the best

CEOs always have peers that they like to compare themselves against. Most of these peers are direct competitors, but often these peers are those that are written up in the business magazines and newspapers. Some of these generic peers include Apple, Google, Procter & Gamble, and Coca Cola, to name a few. Whatever business the CEO fancies as a best-in-class company to emulate, marketing needs to be prepared to show how what they're doing stacks up against them.

Marketers must strive to capture detailed achievement data for both peers and competitors. The knowledge of peer actions and their impact on the consumer and on the competitive environment is critical to developing a complete and functional marketing machine that can be robust and with-stand the test of dynamics in the marketplace.

Marketing planning is out of phase with the customer buying cycle.

As owner of the future, marketing plays a unique role in the organization as it relates to its future success. This is especially true for investment goods, such as white goods, housing and car purchases for consumers, software, machinery with long sales cycles for businesses. If the sales cycle is greater than a month, there is a conspicuous lag between the time the marketing action takes place and the impact it can have on sales. If the sales cycle for high end B2B software takes 6 months, there is nothing the marketing team can do to impact sales next month. This means that if the fiscal year for the sales plan begins in January, the marketing plan needs to begin in July. This offset is extremely difficult for many companies to operate under, but crucial when it comes to executing a successful coordination between marketing activities and sales achievement.

Marketers need to plan top down and bottom up.

At the core of all marketing is the main requirement to focus on the consumer. If the consumer isn't at the core of marketing's decision making, it will never succeed in the long term. This means collecting data at the individual level where possible. On the other hand, depending on the method, marketing analytics can sometimes be more top down, focusing on mass media and the larger marketing activities. To be successful, marketers must focus on the customer while balancing both bottom-up approaches with top-down approaches.

Marketers need a sustainable, repeatable approach.

The best processes in manufacturing are designed for reliability and consistency. They are expected to produce the same results over and over again so that there is little variance from item to item. Any changes to the process need to deliver incremental value, either in terms of cost savings or quality improvements. These changes need to be sustainable, so that they can be depended on day in and day out over long stretches of time. This is especially true when the delivery of the end product or service is highly dependent on manpower as opposed to machine power. Restaurants fall into this category. The end product depends on the fine-tuned, individual contributions of many employees throughout the customer experience. Waffle House provides a great example of how sustainability is fully incorporated into its go-to-market strategy and its customer experience delivery. (See Case Study: Waffle House)

The marketing machine is the epitome of this concept. Marketing must deliver sustainable output that can be counted on to continuously deliver results in the form of revenue and profits without exceeding the media budgets, regardless of the adverse actions of the competition or strong headwinds due to external factors.

Case Study: Waffle House

Waffle House is a gem of a restaurant chain based in the southeast United States with over 1,800 restaurants around the country. They specialize in waffles, but offer a full complement of great tasting, cooked-to-order meals. The company prides itself on great operations and has built its in-restaurant systems and activities to optimize their operations and deliver a consistent customer experience. The company is not a major advertiser, but instead relies on its restaurant street presence, store signage, local face-to-face promotion, and brand heritage to maintain and grow sales and generate profit.

When discussing the concept of the marketing machine, Mr. Bert Thornton, former Chairman of the Board, brought up their internal concept of sustainability. If a marketing or operational action can't be sustained to drive ongoing value, then it won't work or needs to be re-worked. The company has tried advertising to grow sales, but the effects weren't sustainable. They couldn't be easily replicated for all stores across the network or used to consistently generate incremental sales. Advertising was discontinued. Waffle House continues its more tried-and-true marketing through street signage and consistent, sustainable customer experience.

A conversation with Bert Thornton, former Chairman of the Board, Waffle House, December 2016.

Section One:
Marketing Needs to Be a Machine

Chapter 3

What Is a Marketing Machine?

We see machines everywhere. Drones are new machines entering our homes and neighborhoods. They have four motors, four propellers, a frame and a control unit. When properly piloted, they can do amazing things. When a camera is attached, they can capture images and videos that otherwise aren't possible. Whether it's over a whale in the ocean or traversing some cliff in South America, the views and videos are astounding. The pilot moves a lever and the drone ascends; another lever and the drone shifts just slightly to the right.

The marketing machine needs to deliver the same level of astonishment and control. It needs to allow a business to know that when precious corporate dollars—the lever—are invested, they will deliver directly measurable, predictable, and attributable sales and profit; that funds invested in one media channel with one media message with one number of impressions with one timing with a certain frequency will deliver a certain expectation of future sales.

The marketing machine

The marketing machine has three primary components:

1. Vision and planning
2. Scenario building, optimization, and ROI
3. Rolling planning and execution.

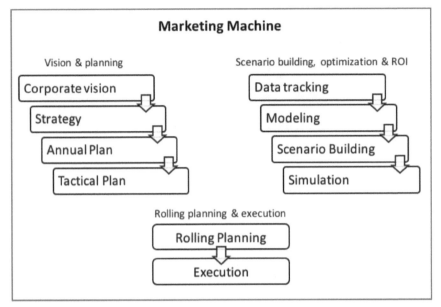

Figure 2: Key Building Blocks of a Marketing Machine

Vision and planning

The *corporate vision* is the driving force behind the company. It is what the CEO develops and maintains. It is what the shareholders invest in. The shareholders see the vision as something that can generate better returns compared to other investments with other companies with comparable risk. Vision planning incorporates how the vision will satisfy consumer demands, compare to the competition, and be brought to market given competitive, channel, and external factors.

The *strategic* plan represents how the company can deliver on the vision, given challenges in the marketplace. It typically covers about 3 to 5 years into the future. The *annual* plan represents the specific actions that will be undertaken, with a specific budget allocation, to achieve those goals specified for the year. As it relates to marketing, these goals consist of a top-line revenue number, a bottom-line profit number, a brand position, and an investment number spread throughout the year based on seasonal changes and other expectations of competitive, channel, or external factors. The *tactical* plan represents the concrete spending actions that will take place in the coming days and weeks with very specific details of how the selling and marketing investments will be made. It is made up of various campaigns—working either singly or across media channels—pricing options, distribution channels, brand attributes, and product features.

Scenario building, optimization, and ROI

Scenario building and optimization incorporate all pertinent data and, through the use of simple and complex models, determine how each selling and marketing action can be optimized to achieve the tactical and annual plan for revenue, profit, and brand position with the highest ROI. Through simulations based on the expected future scenarios, a risk profile is built to assess uncertainties about the future so that the marketing team can achieve the tactical targets with the least investment and most certainty.

Rolling planning and execution

Due to incomplete knowledge of competitive actions, channel factors, and external factors, the actual results of any action in the marketplace are uncertain. As marketing tactics unfold and produce results in the marketplace, these results need to be tracked and adjustments made to be certain that achievement meets or exceeds the corporate plan. By tracking results on a regular, periodic basis, either weekly or monthly, deviations from the plan can be quickly determined and adjustments can be made so that the company has the best chance of achieving the annual plan. It is this process that brings together the plans and targets on the one hand and the ability to execute to them on the other, given the risks and uncertainties in the market.

CEOs need to know these terms:

Attribution – Attribution determines the level of sales or another success factor due to a specific investment in a marketing channel.

Ad Network – An ad network is a method for digital advertisers to bid on the placement of impressions based on specific criteria with available publishers.

Display Ad – A display ad is an ad displayed on a website viewed through a browser on a desktop or mobile device. It can be made up of simple text, an image, an animated image, or a full multimedia production.

Search Terms – Search terms are key words or key phrases entered into a search engine, such as Google or Bing, to find websites that can provide further information related to the search term.

Retargeting – Retargeting allows businesses to continue advertising to visitors to a website by repeating that message to that specific browser (the individual) after they have left the webpage.

Rise of the machine

Digital marketing is leading the revolution in terms of being able to project the future. They can predict with relative accuracy the level of response that can be expected from an investment in search marketing, banner advertising, and/or retargeting. Because of the almost immediate response, the marketer can easily attribute the number of visits to the website and the number of conversions to each of these channels. Various experiments can be run to optimize the investment across each of the channels to make certain that the investment in each of the search terms is worthwhile, that they are running the right display ad across the right ad networks, and that the right creative and the number of retargets delivers the best value for the business.

For the CEO

A/B Testing – Experimental design and A/B testing, pre-post testing, and many other names have been given to this simple marketing effectiveness measurement method. This method simply compares a test marketing activity in a test segment against a control marketing activity (or no marketing activity) with a separate control segment in order to determine whether the two marketing activities had any differential impact and how strong that impact was.

There are many challenges in using A/B testing, but it can be a very effective methodology to determine the effectiveness of media, especially digital media.

As consumers move many of their purchases (and much of their pre-purchase information gathering) to digital platforms, and even more so to mobile platforms, the new levels of available tracking and other treasure troves of information are making the digital platform the method of choice for many marketers. Marketers can easily measure page views, ad views, and click-thrus without even trying. They can run experiments to determine if one creative or one channel works better than another. In fact, marketers are shifting resources away from traditional media channels to digital media channels because they are highly reactive, easily measurable, and relatively inexpensive to get started with. Digital marketing is a deceptively easy way for many businesses to build a machine where the required level of sales can be delivered based on the level of investment.

However, digital channels can only go so far. For certain smaller businesses, they can provide everything that is needed. Yet, for larger businesses they can only reach a certain number of consumers, they can't easily build the brand, or certain segments aren't as active in the digital channel as in other media channels. Larger businesses still need to use traditional, non-digital media channels, such as TV, print, radio, out-of-home, sponsorships, events, and PR. Whereas millennials consume most of their media through digital devices, boomers traditionally still consume a large portion of their media through traditional sources. In order to transform these channels into a machine, marketers need to build marketing models that cover all channels, digital and traditional, to understand how these channels interact with each other to garner the best value across all media investments. These models can be simple or complex, depending on the industry or category and the level of marketing investment of the brand.

Investing in the machine

So many marketing organizations operate despite themselves. Most cannot claim to be a machine. As described in Chapter 2, the reasons are many as to why marketing is broken. Even with the best of intentions, it's often difficult to get a clunky machine humming with that quiet purr of a 12-cylinder Jaguar V12 engine. In fact, there are very few marketing teams that can do this across their media mix. There are egos, silos, and agencies fighting for their turf, their commissions, and their rebates. But if the marketing team is able to get the machine running properly, they can deliver extraordinary growth and opportunities.

Other departments in the organization have been able to overcome the disjointedness in their operations because they have been at it longer. Probably the first to accomplish this was the accounting department. They implemented accounting systems because it was so important to make certain that cash was properly and accurately tracked. Of course, the government wanted its cut too, so to report earnings and potentially reduce taxes the accounting team built sophisticated systems to track revenues, expenses, and investments. Then came the manufacturing department with their enterprise resource management systems. Then came the customer service teams with CRM and service management systems that easily tracked and reported their exact service quality levels. One of the last groups was the sales force. Salesforce automation systems have now been implemented throughout most organizations, providing great business flow tracking for the entire selling function. For large corporations, SAP[5] provides enterprise-level software and automation touching just about every function in the organization. It's now marketing's turn.

With the advent of digital marketing and its phenomenal success, marketers have been shifting investments out of traditional media and into online media at an ever-expanding pace. Print, radio, and outdoor advertising, among others, have correspondingly declined. They are starting to recover, but have easily lost half of their former strength. With digital advertising, marketing automation and tracking are now becoming *de rigeur*.

Right and Left-brained People

Right-brained people are typically more creative, or artistic, whereas left-brained are more logical and numbers-oriented. Most marketing creative people consider themselves to be more right-brained and therefore have an aversion to numbers.

In the past, marketers have shunned measurement because they felt that creative development was at the core of all successful marketing; they can't be creative if they have to worry about the numbers. Right- and left-brained marketing was not possible. Now creative teams are finding that even great creative may not make for the best email subject line, google AdWords ad, or Facebook-promoted post. A/B testing and being creative in testing,

---

[5] www.SAP.com, October 2016.

especially across multiple dimensions at the same time, is what drives marketing success, even with a great creative concept.

Marketing automation found in digital channels needs to be replicated across all traditional media channels. Marketers need be able to see the interim responses from their efforts, model them, and then make valid predictions based on their best estimates of the competition and the external situation that will be facing the company in the short and medium term. This will allow them to react much earlier than the next planning cycle and significantly earlier than the annual planning cycle. It also means the CEO and CFO need to provide them the leeway so they can spend more when necessary to make certain that, in the face of a competitive action or response, the company and the brand can still make their numbers without exceeding their overall budgets. This process requires that the team is trained to develop and exercise their ability to peer into the future. It requires them to develop potential scenarios of what might happen and to come up with potential responses that can be tested *before* they're implemented in the marketplace. This process requires new thinking in how the marketing team approaches their activations in the marketplace.

It first requires a marketing machine that can take fuel in and spit out fully manufactured gadgets. The marketing machine takes in creative concepts and investments in media channels and (with the right conveyor belts) delivers sales out. Inside the marketing machine, the conveyor belts are tracked and sized based on a functioning marketing model. The model determines the relative impact of each media channel on interim factors, such as clicks to a website, or footfall to an auto dealership, and then how they combine to deliver consumer purchases. Each media activity in each media channel is tempered by brand attributes, price, distribution and competitive activities, and channel and external factors.

The marketing machine

Industrial machines have input materials, energy, controls, and outputs. They have manpower watching over them and making adjustments or repairs when necessary. Subassembly lines create partial assemblies that get built across multiple machines into the final product. The products get packaged and finally shipped.

Similarly, marketing needs to take in energy in the form of investment to spur working media. The creative process can be likened to the design (the intellectual property) of the machine and the layout of the production line. It's similar to the tools and dies necessary to stamp out new gadgets. Measuring success throughout the assembly process at different points in the assembly line measures the quality of manufacturing. In marketing, this comprises the measurement of interim factors such as unique visitors, clicks, conversions, brand imagery, and others.

The marketing machine must allow the company to invest more or less working media to generate an increase or decrease in sales. Investing in additional working media should deliver more sales volume. However, too much investment starts to deliver less and less. There will be diminishing returns. For smaller companies, the problems can work in reverse. Because the company has been inconsistently advertising, or because they just haven't been able to spend enough, there may be no breakthrough. Their ads are not able to get above the clutter to begin to elicit a meaningful level of response. Once they do jump above the clutter, their ads start to become very effective.

The marketing machine is a model of the connection between the inputs and the outputs: the media expenditures on the one side and the number of gadgets sold on the other. For example, a model might indicate that an input of $1 million in television advertising leads to $15 million in sales volume over the following 3 months. It might also indicate that the $1 million in television advertising will increase unique visits to the website and $2 million in sales through the online store. It might also indicate that $100,000 in promoted posts on Facebook delivers an incremental $3 million in sales in the online store and $1 million in brick and mortar stores. The marketing machine determines that when the Facebook campaign and television advertising are run simultaneously, the Facebook campaign is improved by 14%. It determines that when the competition advertises, sales decrease by 3%. The marketing machine incorporates all of these relationships among marketing actions, combinatorial or synergistic effects between media channels, effects of price and distribution, effects of competitive marketing activities, and finally channel and external factors, such as the weather, interest rates, and unemployment. At its core, the marketing machine incorporates a marketing model that is accurate and predictable to help marketers understand marketing effectiveness and ROI in the past, and project marketing effectiveness in the future. It is predictive and accountable and can accurately simulate the future.

Diminishing returns

Diminishing returns means that for each additional message inserted into the market, a lower and lower incremental response will be achieved. For example, if we insert 100 messages into the market we may sell 75 units. However, if we insert 200 messages into the market, we may only sell 135 units for an increase of only 60 units. If 300 messages are inserted into the market, only 185 units would be sold, for an increase of only 50 units. In other words, the first 100 messages delivered 75 units, but the second additional 100 messages only delivered 60 units. Then the third additional 100 messages only delivered 50 units. The response diminished for each increment of messages inserted.

This plays out in many systems, including digital impressions purchased or the total marketing investment. If there were an infinite number of customers and if all messages were able to be equally seen by a portion of those customers, then we would expect that each additional message would deliver the same level of sales. But in reality there are a limited number of consumers, some people will see a message more than once, and others may never see any messages. If it takes more than one message to lead to a purchase, then each incremental message will lead to less and less possible returns. This is diminishing returns.

The 4P3CEIF data framework

Marketing models have many potential inputs. Here is the consumer data framework we've found to be most successful:

- Our 4 Ps – Product (including brand imagery and brand perceptions), Price (including total cost of ownership), Place (such as brick and mortar stores or online e-commerce; shelf location) and Promotion (all messages inserted into the marketplace) for our brand
- The 3 Cs
    - Competitive 4 Ps – As above, but for peers in the same market
    - The Consumer
        - Consumer trial and repeat behavior

- Consumer progress down the purchase funnel, moving from awareness to interest, desire and action (AIDA)[6]
- Consumer acquisition, retention, and churn behavior
- Consumer segmentation
- Consumer purchase behavior
- Consumer shopping behavior
- Consumer preferences and need states
  - The Channel
    - Channel segmentation and consumer channel preferences
    - Channel factors
- External factors – Interest rates, unemployment, technology availability, government regulation, and many more
- Interim factors – Web visits and online behavior, social behavior, leads generated, and many more
- Financial success – Sales volumes and revenues by product, region, or other critical success factors

---

For the CEO

Brand Attributes – Brand attributes are mutually exclusive attributes that consumers perceive about all brands in a category or industry. Example attributes can be: "This brand is recommended by doctors," "This brand is healthy for my child," or "This is a brand for people like me."

Channel Factors – Channel factors represent overall trends taking place in the distribution channel. For example, the trend shifting shopping away from traditional trade to modern trade, or the trend of shifting purchases to online stores from brick and mortar.

External Factors – External Factors are outside of the control of the competitors and distribution channels operating in the marketplace. They include the weather, interest rates, unemployment rates and changes in government regulation.

---

[6] See Priyanka, R., "AIDA Marketing Communication Model: Stimulating a purchase decision in the minds of the consumers through a linear progression of steps," *International Journal of Multidisciplinary Research in Social Management*, Vol. 1, 2013, pp 37-44

Our 4 Ps and competitive 4 Ps

All aspects of how a consumer perceives a brand are described in the 4 Ps. Consumers purchase a Product with emotional and rational attributes at a Price (compared to other prices) in a distribution channel (Place) after having experienced product or brand messages (Promotion) either in the store, in the home, or outside the home. Although other marketing theorists may have other Ps, we've always found these four to be at the core of everything related to the relationship a consumer has with the product/brand.

All competitors' products and brands in the market are similarly specified through these same 4 Ps.

For the CEO
Consumer v. Customer v. Shopper

Businesses are consumers too. Businesses consume products, so throughout the book the term consumer can mean both an individual or a business. Customers are generally those that actually pay for the product. Consumers may not directly pay the business for the product, but may pay a retailer for the product and then consume at home. In this case the retailer is the customer.

Shoppers are the people that actually purchase the product. They may purchase it for their consumption or for the consumption by others.

The consumer

Consumer trial and repeat behavior

With recently introduced products, consumers may or may not have ever purchased that brand or from that company before. The first time a product is purchased by a consumer is defined as a trial. The second and following purchases are defined as a repeat. After a handful of repeats, the following purchases are generally considered to be regular purchases.

Consumer progress down the purchase funnel, moving from awareness to interest, desire and action (AIDA)[7]

The purchase funnel was designed to help marketers determine where and what types of messages are most appropriate to generate sales for the company. A newly launched brand needs to invest in advertising messages and channels that can drive awareness whereas an existing brand with very high awareness may need to focus messages on building the brand or building purchase intent. AIDA (Awareness, Interest, Desire, Action) is a construct called the purchase funnel that was developed to represent the location consumers as they move from not being aware, to developing interest, desire (brand preference) and then finally action.

Consumer acquisition, retention, and churn behavior

In industries where there is a direct relationship between the buyer and the seller and where products or services have a long lifecycle, such as, new homes or new cars, it's important to track and model what generated the initial acquisition of the customer, what types of things were helpful in retaining the customer, and what led to churn (attrition).

Mini Case Study: Churn

Through deep marketing analytics a natural gas utility was able to determine the drivers of churn for their residential consumers. With this knowledge, the company was able to improve their service levels in key areas along with the messaging around these service areas to reduce long term churn rates from 5% to 4%. This led to an enormous gain in overall revenue.

Churn and attrition are defined as when it can be confirmed that consumers have switched out of your service for the competition, such as with a gas utility or a wireless mobile service provider.

---

[7] Ibid.

> **Mini Case Study: Segmentation**
>
> A major online website with 100s of millions of members, whose revenue was generated primarily through advertising, was able to improve the ability of their advertisers to segment the site's members into many micro-segments. This improved micro-segmentation led to an increase in over 50% in advertising effectiveness for the site's advertisers.

Consumer segmentation

Consumers can act very differently at an individual level, but large groups of consumers mimic the actions of like consumers and thus can be grouped into segments. The consumers in a segment have many like characteristics, demographics, and behaviors. Segmentation dimensions can be based on demographics (such as age, gender, marital status), firmographics (such as company size, number of employees), psychographics (such as interests and lifestyles) and many others. Segmentation dimensions are critical to understanding consumer behavior and capitalizing on that behavior to offer product variants, pricing strategies, and marketing communications to each segment. With new online data sets becoming available every day, segmentation and targeting options are many.

Consumer purchase behavior

Knowing how consumers make purchase decisions must be at the heart of the marketing model. If we can understand the consumer purchase decision process we can better understand how our marketing can deliver incremental value to that process and increase the likelihood that our products will be purchased over those of the competition.

Consumer shopping behavior

Consumers have different shopping behavior. Some individual consumers go shopping once a week, planning out the purchases with a shopping list. Others go shopping every day and purchase only what they need for that day's consumption. Some shoppers make purchase decisions for the entire family based on their understanding of the preferences of each of the family members.

Simple business supplies may be purchased by an administrative assistant ordering what is needed and when it is needed for his/her coworkers. These purchases often resemble consumer shopping behavior. On the other hand, large businesses generally shop with a purchase committee, especially for major investment purchases, for which prospective suppliers go through a rigorous and lengthy purchase process.

Consumer preferences

Consumers have preferences for certain functional and emotional attributes in a product. One consumer may prefer low-sugar carbonated beverages. Others may prefer low-caffeine drinks. One consumer may prefer that their infant formula be a brand recommended by doctors, others may prefer the brand that is perceived as good value for money. It is these functional and emotional preferences of brand attributes that determine which brand will be more likely to be chosen at which price.

Consumer need states

Consumers have certain need states. If the company is moving in thirty days, they need to quickly choose their new broadband communications provider. If the company is expected to grow when they win a new contract, they may simply want to add to their current broadband communications bandwidth through their existing provider. Consumers at a baseball game may want a beer, whereas others at the same game want the beer, but because they are the designated driver, will purchase a non-alcoholic beverage. Each of these consumers are in different need states as they relate to the product under consideration.

The channel

Channel segmentation and consumer channel preferences

Consumers shop at different channels for different reasons. Some consumers purchase aluminum siding from a DIY[8] store, others purchase the same siding from a contractor who will install it for them. Some consumers will shop for days on end seeking out the best price, others will simply purchase

---

[8] DIY: Do it yourself

the same item quickly from the first available source due to convenience. Each retail store offers a different value for the consumer as the consumer purchases the products they seek based on their individual preferences and circumstance. These circumstances may also change based on the time of day or day of the week. During grocery shopping a can of Coca Cola will be purchased at a mass marketer because the price is the lowest, but that same can of Coke will be purchased at a relatively expensive convenience store when the consumer is on the road getting gas.

Along the same lines, some businesses may prefer to purchase products at the lowest cost from a no-frills supplier, where others may prefer to have the solution fully integrated, installed, and maintained by a full-service value-added reseller.

Channel factors

There are dynamics in each channel that need to be built into the model as trends change the way consumers and businesses make purchases. The rise of modern trade supplanting traditional mom-and-pop stores throughout Asia, for example, may change the way consumers make their purchase decisions. Similarly, if online shopping offers free shipping and the convenience of shopping at home, the local brick-and-mortar stores may go out of business.

External factors

External factors are those factors that influence purchases in the category, but are generally outside of the control of the competitors and channel partners in the category or industry. These can be interest rates, changes in government regulations, the weather, and many others. Some of these can be predicted or known in advance, for example, the date a new regulation goes into effect or the availability of new technology may be well known and fully expected. Others are totally stochastic, such as the weather. In most cases, external factors impact the total demand in the category, affecting each brand equally; however, in some cases external factors may only affect a few brands, such as the boycott of French wines in the early 2000s in the U.S.

Europe and Personal Data Protection Regulation

The European Union just passed a series of personal data protection regulations known as the GDPR: General Data Protection Regulation. It is slated to go into effect in May 2018. It provides a framework of how advertisers need to track use, permissions, and sources of personal data in order to provide a higher level of consumer privacy in the digital age throughout Europe. It affects any advertiser wishing to use digital channels to access consumers within the European Union. This new regulation and others like it will continue to ratchet down the value of personalized digital advertising, having a long-term impact on the overall effectiveness of the online advertising channel. More information can be found at: http://cdn2.hubspot.net/hubfs/329382/GDPR_eBook.pdf?t=1476440677243, October 2016

Interim factors

There are many types of interim factors. These can include store visit counts, web visits, brand imagery, sales leads, and others. They generally help the company to track the impact of their marketing, especially in longer sales cycle industries, such as home buying, business software, or vacation travel. Interim factors differ from KPIs because KPIs are directly related to performance, whereas the interim factors are slightly more general. KPIs are used to manage the business and are typically limited in number to the measurement of short term performance. Interim metrics come from various sources and may be useable to answer certain types of business questions.

Financial success

Sales by product, by variant, by SKU, by brand, by region, by segment, by sales channel, or by other dimension are critical to track in order to gain the most accurate and predictive model. Sales unit volumes and dollar volumes are key elements to understanding what was sold and at what price it was sold. It is important to differentiate between sell-in, and sell-through (see the call out box: Sell-in, Sell-Through, Installation, and Use). For consumer industries, there are a handful of syndicated research companies providing this detailed sell-through data, such as Nielsen, GfK, and J.D. Power.

Sell-in, Sell-Through, Installation, and Use

Marketers must work at many levels throughout the purchase funnel. Retailers work to generate sales. Their internal systems provide easy statistics as to what was sold on an hourly or daily basis. This is what consumers have purchased. It is often likened to consumption, although consumption typically takes place after the shopper gets home and the product is put in use, or "consumed," by members of the household. For consumer goods, manufacturers' products are sold into the channel, defined as **sell-in**. This is an important statistic for the channel sales team, but not for the consumer marketer. The consumer marketer wants to know when the product is purchased by the consumer from the retailer, defined as **sell-through**.

Software companies are interested in sell-through, as well as **installation** and **use**. For large enterprise software providers selling corporate licenses, the software may be automatically installed on an end-user's desktop computer, but it may not actually be used. The enterprise software provider needs to make sure the sale takes place, the installation takes place, and finally actual usage takes place. This is especially true for software providers looking to reduce their support costs of older versions of their software. They want the latest version to be sold, installed, and used by their corporate customers to reduce customer service issues and increase customer satisfaction.

Modeling methods

Once all the data streams have been determined and the most influential and important data streams have been captured in an accurate and timely fashion, a predictive model can be built to show how these data streams lead to corporate success. In an ideal world, all data streams would be measured from the perspective of the consumer. It would be incorrect or misleading if sales, for example, were measured via sell-in to the distribution channel as opposed to sell-through to the consumer. The data streams must, as best as possible, align to the actual timing of the consumer purchase decision.

There are several methods to building a marketing model. CEOs should demand effective models from their marketing teams since with a successful predictive model, marketing can deliver predictability and accountability. This in turn can reduce company risk. Because the marketing model is at the core of the marketing machine, it is important to understand the inherent risks and uncertainties associated with marketing models. Described below are five popular methods to model the impact of media and build a predictive marketing model:

1. Attribution Modeling (last touch attribution, last click attribution, algorithmic attribution, and others)
2. Experimental Design
3. Predictive Analytics
4. Marketing Mix Modeling (statistical)
5. Agent-Based Modeling & Simulation

Attribution modeling

Attribution Modeling measures the direct impact of a particular media channel on some interim result. In an ideal world, it would measure both the direct and indirect impact of a marketing action on sales. Offline, the direct impact can be measured through offer codes, promotion codes, coupon codes, or marketing response codes. Each of these codes confirms that the purchaser saw the specific advertisement and made a purchase, confirmed through the entry and tracking of the code.

In the digital world, this can also include the use of specifically designed landing pages and other means to tie the marketing action to some directly measurable consumer action and result. Just about every digital marketing activity has some ability to measure the direct result of the digital media activity. The simplest method is to track and count the sources of clicks and visits to a website. In a more advanced way, clicks can be tagged so that the visitor's behavior can be followed throughout the site. Additional methods include placing cookies on the browser that can be tracked. In many cases tracking and measurement can be triggered through the placement of invisible pixels on a web page to trigger the tracking mechanism. In this way consumer click behaviors can be accurately tracked, measured, and attributed.

This method works well if the conversion (sale) occurs quickly after the initial digital media activity, but needs to be enhanced if the sales cycle is long or if the sale takes place offline. If a store is trying to measure the impact of digital media on generating in-store sales, there needs to be a method to measure the connection between digital media and website visits. Then there needs to be some measurement between site visits and physical store visits, and then there needs to be some connection between store visits and transactions and possibly transaction value or shopping basket size.

Attribution modeling and structured equation modeling

Let's assume an insurance company would like to measure the impact of search engine marketing (for example purchasing AdWords on the Google search engine) on incremental sales. They have designed their web page with a landing page for each of their search terms. On the landing pages are forms that the insurance seeker would fill out for a further call and appointment setting.

1. First, the company needs to determine the connection between impressions purchased and landing page visits. Let's say they purchase 100,000 impressions and receive a click-thru rate of 0.7%. They receive 700 visitors to their landing pages, but only 300 fill out forms. Their click thru rate is 0.7%, but their conversion rate at this stage is 0.3%.
2. Second, they now need to determine the number of appointments that actually take place. Let's say 65% or 195.
3. Third they need to determine the number of insurance policies (and policy value) that are eventually sold over the course of the next several months or other limited timeframe. Let's say they are able to sign up 25% or 49 policies worth $40,000 in annual premiums.

In summary, they purchased 100,000 impressions on Google AdWords and were able to generate 49 new policies worth an average of $40,000 in annual premiums. If this were able to be very consistent and predictable and had a positive ROI, it would be a great method to generate incremental revenue.

Structured equation modeling in this simple example helps the marketer to define the relationships between search impressions and landing page visits, between landing page visits and filled forms, between filled forms and set appointments, and between completed appointments and policies sold. If these conversion rates between each link in the sales cycle chain are consistent across different media channels and consumer segments, structured equation modeling can be very successful at helping the marketing analyst predict sales volumes for each media channel and providing a way to predict sales and potentially optimize sales for a given level of investment. However, complexities must also be considered since diminishing returns, an economic downturn, competitive advertising, or even the positive impacts of our own simultaneous television advertising can also influence the click-thru and conversion rates.

There are several types of attribution modeling:

- **Last touch or last click attribution** which counts the last touch as the sole contributor to the consumer action. Last touch can be in any media, whereas last click attribution typically refers to a digital environment where a specific click leads to a measurable consumer action.

- **First touch or first click attribution** counts and tracks the first time a consumer clicks on an ad.
- **Weighted attribution or algorithmic attribution** weights all of the different clicks associated with the consumer actions in such a way as to provide a more accurate picture of the value of several, parallel digital media channels on the consumer action.

Unfortunately, most attribution methods ignore any parallel *non*-digital marketing activities. If there was a price drop, or if there was a TV campaign running in parallel, most attribution modeling methods will not capture the contributions of these activities.

Experimental design

Experimental design runs scientific tests to determine the impact of media. This method can be very effective in measuring impact, since if executed properly experimental design can easily isolate the impact of a single media channel. Experimental design has many names, such as A/B testing, test/control group testing, and pre/post testing. For websites with a large number of visitors, many tests can be run to determine the effectiveness of very specific marketing actions with very reliable results. For example, if the design of a website needs to be optimized, different creative designs can be tested to determine which design leads to a higher level of conversion. Website design tests can include the location of the company logo, the background color of the site, or the location and discount level of a special offer. The marketing team no longer needs to argue with the creative designer as to what constitutes a more effective design. Testing can now provide the answer.

> **Experimental design contamination**
>
> Let's assume a company wants to test the impact of mass media advertising in China by advertising in two test cities, Shanghai and Guangzhou, and comparing their results to a control city (Beijing) where there is no advertising.
>
> If Shanghai and Guangzhou increase sales by 15% more during the campaign period than the level of sales in the control city of Beijing, then a reasonable assumption is that the advertising delivered a 15% increase in sales. If the sales in Beijing didn't increase at all, then this would be an uncontaminated result. But what if sales increased in Beijing during the campaign period as well, let's say by 5%? Questions to be answered include, what could have caused this increase? Could the increase be due to some seasonal fluctuation? Could it be due to some random undetermined effect? Could it be due to a spillover effect from the advertising in Shanghai that was designed to be local in nature, but also had some national exposure?
>
> These uncertainties color the predictability of the method for some media channels and provide some level of uncertainty in the answer.

Using experimental design, a test can be set up to present an offer of free shipping to one group of visitors and an offer of 15% off to another. By carefully controlling how these offers are presented and making certain that during the test period the offer is always presented to the same web visitors and there is no leakage between visitor groups, the marketer can determine which offer delivers the highest number of conversions versus the cost of the offer. In this way, marketing can easily optimize web design and better understand how consumers respond to different designs and offers.

Experimental design can be used with just about every media channel, however, there are a handful of critical caveats that need to be followed in order to provide valid, robust results that can be depended on to make confident marketing decisions. (These aren't presented here but are available in the link in the footnote.[9]) The most challenging include running a test with a statistically significant number of samples for a valid test and keeping the testing environment from being contaminated as discussed in the sidebars.

---

[9] There are many sources in the literature to help with understanding these caveats, such as http://people.vetmed.wsu.edu/jmgay/courses/GlossExpDesign.htm, October 2016.

Experimental design and sample size

One of the biggest issues with experimental design is how to choose a sample size that is sufficiently large to provide statistical confidence that the answer delivered represents the true impact due to the media. In almost every case it is larger than we would like it to be.

For example, a measured increase in sales of 5% in 10 samples may actually be 25% when measured across 1,000 samples. Defining the test with a proper sample size is critical to getting the best results.

Predictive analytics

Predictive analytics is a misnomer. For the layman, this analytic method as it is named here would generally be understood to predict customer response to a marketing activity. In this case the term is correct, but all of the other methods mentioned here are also designed to determine the response to a specific marketing activity. Predictive analytics in the parlance of marketing analytics refers to analytics used to determine when customers might purchase an upgrade or some additional product, or when they might churn and leave to purchase the same product or service from a competitor. It is used to determine which marketing activities can potentially influence that upsell or mitigate the risk of a pending churn.

Predictive analytics then refers to the underlying methodology used to determine these connections. The statistical methodology is typically based on logistic regression modeling. Instead of predicting the upsell or churn, logistic regression predicts the *probability* of an individual customer to churn or be upsold. Once the model is complete, the outputs of a logistic regression model can then determine the linkage between an investment in some marketing activity and its ability to reduce the probability of churn or increase the likelihood to upsell.

Marketing mix modeling (MMM)

Marketing mix modeling is also a misnomer. In the parlance of marketing analytics, it generally means the determination of impact of all the contributors to incremental sales using statistical regression analysis. However, any of the 5 methods mentioned here can be used to build a marketing mix model.

Marketing mix modeling was initially used by major brands about 30 years ago. It is a very successful methodology to link mass media—such as TV, radio, and print—to incremental sales. The assumption is that if there is television advertising in a specific week and there is a sales increase in that particular week, the two are likely linked. If this happens consistently over a modeling period of 2 or 3 years (104 or 156 weeks), then the assumption is that television is directly linked to all the increases in all the weeks that television was present. This process is repeated for all media channels, pricing actions, levels of distribution, and external factors to determine the relative incremental impact for each of the contributors to incremental sales volume. In this way, the average incremental impact of a specific media investment to sales can now be determined. Marketing mix modeling is widely used by most major brands; this methodology can be used not only to determine the contribution of marketing to sales, but also to many other factors, such as visits to a web site or likes to a Facebook page.

Agent-based modeling & simulation (ABMS)

Agent-based modeling and simulation takes a very different approach to modeling the impact of marketing and external factors on sales. "Agents" are defined as virtual representations of individuals or groups of consumers in the software. This allows an agent-based model to provide highly consumer centric insights into a particular category or industry. Agent-based models have two major differences from all other methods:

1. Agent-based models are based on a framework of how marketers believe consumers make purchase decisions. For example, a consumer can't purchase a product if they aren't aware of the brand or the product. They can't purchase the product if it is not found on the shelf in the store when they go shopping. If an ad is presented to a consumer, there is some likelihood that they will become aware, build purchase intent, and/or build brand preference.

2. Agent-based models are calibrated such that a simulation run of the model with real inputs generates simulated outputs with as little

error as possible when compared to actual outputs. Whereas in a statistical model the linkages between marketing activities and sales are determined through a mathematical process using statistics, a simulation process estimates the linkages by running hundreds or thousands of simulations to estimate what the best linkage coefficients are for each stage of the consumer purchase process. Once these linkage coefficients are determined, the model is defined as being calibrated. It can now be used to accurately simulate the impact of marketing activities and external factors on consumer purchase behavior.

Agent-based modeling and new product launch

All other analytic methods have difficulties with optimizing a new product launch, because they depend on past market data about the product. With a new product launch this data doesn't exist. For most modeling methods, such as marketing mix modeling, about 12 months or data would be required to build a model of the new product in order to make future projections for that.

Agent-based modeling is very different. Because it is built on a framework of how consumers make purchase decisions, the model has been defined to know how consumers respond to various prices, to various brand imageries and so on. Because of this, the model knows how a consumer will respond to the new product, because the model knows how consumers have responded in the past to other combinations of brand imagery, price, distribution and advertising. In this way, an agent-based model can be built to provide more insight, not only into static markets, but also into highly dynamic markets where products are being launched or retired, new sales channels are being developed or major new external factors might come into play.

Because an agent-based model is built on a framework of how consumers make purchase decisions, marketers can use it to deduce how to improve their marketing with much greater insight. They can determine whether sales can be increased by building the brand, building purchase intent, or by increasing awareness. They can now optimize with much more clarity a new product or brand launch, where there is no prior history of the brand in the marketplace. (See Agent-based modeling and new product launch below).

Now that we understand how to build a marketing model where we put money in and get sales out, we can optimize the marketing mix, make significantly better strategic and tactical marketing decisions, and take the first steps to building a marketing machine.

Marketing ROI, ROMI, mROMI: Simplifying the communication of marketing success

Marketers and marketing analysts have developed a series of communications tools to improve the way the marketing team and the entire company talks about marketing success. There are 3 terms in particular that are important to this discussion: ROMI, mROMI, and Marketing ROI. Each of these definitions help to communicate with clarity and simplicity whether a marketing program is working and how it benchmarks against other marketing channels.

ROMI (Return on Marketing Investment)

Return on marketing investment (ROMI) is calculated by taking the incremental revenue due to a marketing activity and dividing by the incremental marketing investment. If a $1m investment is made on a digital campaign and it contributes $5m in incremental revenue, then the ROMI factor or index is 5.0.

$$\text{ROMI} = \frac{\text{Incremental Revenue}}{\text{Incremental Marketing Investment}}$$

ROMI = $5m/$1m
ROMI = 5.0

mROMI – margin Return on Marketing Investment

Margin return on marketing investment (mROMI) is defined as the incremental profit margin due to a marketing activity divided by the incremental marketing investment. Profit margin is typically provided by the finance department. It can have many names, such as standard margin or operating margin, but is used here as the incremental profit in percent of sales generated from the next unit sold. If the profit margin percentage is 60%, then that same $1m investment contributes $5m in incremental revenue, which, at a

47

60% margin, contributes $3m in incremental profit margin. In this case the mROMI factor or index is = 3.0.

$$\text{mROMI} = \frac{\text{Incremental Revenue * Profit Margin \%}}{\text{Incremental Marketing Investment}}$$

mROMI = $3m / $1m
mROMI = 3.0

Or even more simply stated, the mROMI is simply the ROMI multiplied by the variable profit margin percentage. An mROMI of 1.0 is a marketing investment delivering no profit or loss: a break-even investment.

$$\text{mROMI} = \text{ROMI * Profit Margin \%}$$

In most cases, at least within the marketing department, the ROMI or mROMI factors are accurate enough to make great decisions. If, for example, the ROMI for TV is 3.0 and the ROMI for digital is 5.0, then an investment in digital provides more revenue, and therefore some of the TV budget should be reallocated to digital.

Similarly, if the mROMI for social is 8.0 and the mROMI for digital is 3.0, then the amount of profit generated from social is better than digital and therefore some of the digital budget should be reallocated to social.

Marketing ROI – Marketing ROI (Return on Investment)

Marketing ROI is a more financially centric communications term, intended to be used with other investments made outside of marketing. Let's assume a gadget manufacturing company has a cost of capital of 12%. That is, an investment of the next dollar in the company will cost the company 12% per year. If, for that company, the return on investment of a new gadget-making machine can be calculated based on various assumptions to deliver an ROI of 23%, which is higher than the cost of capital (12%), then this would be a good investment. These are the typical methods the finance team uses to look at the value of various investments based on estimates of future profits from these investments. Marketing ROI is very similar to the ROI defined above and uses a very similar formula. Marketing ROI is defined as the percent return generated in profit from an incremental marketing investment.

Marketing ROI

$$\text{Marketing ROI} = \frac{(\frac{\text{Incremental Revenue * Profit Margin \%}}{\text{-Incremental Marketing Investment}})\text{*100\%}}{\text{Incremental Marketing Investment}}$$

Marketing ROI = (($5m * 60% — $1m) / $1m) * 100%
Marketing ROI = 200%
mROMI = 3.0

The marketing ROI for the example above would be 200%.

More simply, marketing ROI can be calculated from the mROMI factor as follows:

$$\text{Marketing ROI} = (\text{mROMI-1}) * 100\%$$

It is critical in all these calculations to use incremental revenue due to incremental marketing investment. Unless done carefully, using the total marketing investment or the total revenue may provide erroneous results or may not answer the business question posed.

With these three terms, ROMI, mROMI, and marketing ROI, marketers can now easily compare various marketing investments to optimize their media plans—and they can now communicate them clearly and succinctly within the organization.

Additional applications of the ROMI concept

ROMI can be used for interim metrics as well. For example, if a $10,000 investment in social advertising activity delivers 2,500 Facebook likes, then the $\text{ROMI}_{\text{Facebook Likes}}$ = 0.25 likes per dollar. Each dollar invested in this social advertising activity generates 0.25 likes. It can also be used for units sold per marketing dollar invested. For example, if the marketing investment is $250,000 and 2,000 units were sold, the $\text{ROMI}_{\text{Units sold}}$ = 8.0 units per thousand dollars invested. Each thousand dollars invested in this company sells 8 units.

In the example shown in Case Study: ROMI Factors for a Consumer Packaged Goods Company, print advertising is very successful, generating $4.80 in profit for every dollar invested. On the other hand, billboards only generate $1.00 for every dollar invested. It only breaks even. In this case, unless billboard advertising can be improved, money should be reallocated from billboards to print.

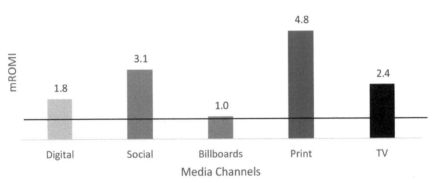

mROMI by Media Channel

Case Study: ROMI Factors for a Consumer Packaged Goods Company

The marketing machine continuum

Marketers have gone through many stages of sophistication. Early on, marketers would advertise and sales would increase. This worked for quite some time, but then it started to work less and less. Competitors started advertising and success metrics needed to be improved. Marketers needed to determine why it wasn't working so well. Then they started asking around and they received anecdotal evidence as to why their advertising wasn't working as well as expected. The anecdotal research was later formalized and made into a full-blown systematic approach to success measurement. Models were developed. Digital media came along and everything was measurable, but there was so much data, marketers needed to figure out how to tease out the most important metrics and make split-second decisions. Attribution models were developed, but they didn't integrate with their traditional media models and sales was still not included.

Sophisticated marketers are finally putting everything together—online analytics, traditional media analytics, and sales analytics—and they're beginning to incorporate planning workflows to tie the corporate vision to the strategic plan to the annual planning process and the tactical execution process. They are working with real-time measurement to stay on track, respond to disruptions, and optimize their responses. They are master marketing mechanics. Below are five levels of marketing mechanics, with the top level being the marketing master mechanics:

Marketing Machine Continuum

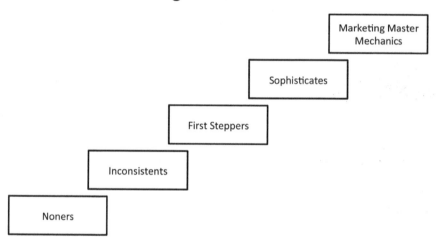

Figure 3: The Marketing Machine Continuum

Noners

Noners are marketing teams characterized through the determination of marketing success through gut feel and anecdotal evidence. If any advertising is undertaken, the management team sees increased sales and attribute scores due to that advertising, but nothing more is done with that information. There are few companies falling in this category, but they certainly exist historically. Today even most small and recently launched companies, because of the inexpensive and easy ways to measure online advertising, do not fall into this category.

Moving out of this category simply requires any level of measurement and analysis. This is the baseline group, which to a large extent barely exists any more.

The inconsistents

For many small businesses and many B2B marketers, measuring marketing is a challenge. Marketing is done inconsistently and, because of that, there is little consistent measurement. Managers know they need to do some marketing and that it can be a source of growth for the company, but they can't find a way to invest in marketing that can provide dependable, tangible results. Because of this, they also don't have a systematic way to measure the impact of marketing through to the conversion. They are measuring leads generated, website visits, and Facebook likes, but aren't putting these measurements into a coherent view of how their marketing is working. With these inconsistent methods and seemingly lackluster results, the company continually reverts back to investments in the sales and business development team. Although the sales team is always conceptually part of marketing, in this case it is also viewed as the only source of business, yet still challenged to work at its fullest sales potential. Small B2B companies with one or two salespersons and small consumer companies, such as mom-and-pop consumer retailers, fall into this category.

Moving to the next level for these companies is no small task. Because their level of marketing investment is small, being able to spend enough to make the measurement meaningful enough and accurate enough requires a breakout in disposable cash to successfully invest in marketing and marketing measurement. With this first seed investment, the company can finally track some success to marketing and feel confident that the marketing investments are worth it and deliver real value to growing the business.

First steppers

First steppers have moved to being able to consistently measure the success of key aspects of their marketing. They aren't measuring their marketing mix fully, but have some of the major elements measured and in some cases, have determined a positive ROI. The measurement and calculations aren't fully systematized, but the company is investing in marketing and in measurement and starting to guide its marketing investments accordingly. Many large B2B marketers with small- to medium-sized sales teams fall into this level on the continuum. Many small consumer marketers spending less than $1M in media also fall into this category.

These marketers have begun to use attribution-based measurements, as well as experimental design, to inform their marketing decision-making. For B2B marketers, this means they are measuring the impact of sales and understanding how investments in sales work, and how investments in marketing can support their sales activities.

These marketers may not be spending enough in marketing to fully move to the next level, but as they grow they improve all aspects of their sales and marketing investments based on data and simple analytics. Moving to the next level may require a larger marketing budget to properly afford more sophisticated measurement and analytics, but the management team and marketing team have the wherewithal to make these improvements when the time comes.

Measure 80% of the budget or 80% of the impact?

It's typically considered prudent to focus on the top expense items in the marketing budget because this is generally where the concerns from outside the marketing department originate. The finance team has an ingrained habit of focusing on the top expense items. Unless the CEO came up through the ranks out of marketing, they too focus on the top expense items.

This is not the right way. Although they often overlap, the marketing team needs to focus not just on high cost items but on the media channels contributing the most revenue. If 1% of the media budget generates 20% of the revenue and 50% of the budget generates 40% of the revenue, then these two need to be at the top of the list. Remember, the sales team always focuses on the largest revenue accounts, not necessarily the most profitable accounts first.

For the CEO
Mass marketing versus one-to-one marketing

One-to-one marketing defines the marketing process when the customer is uniquely known. Utilities, mobile service providers, and others have a direct relationship with the customer. Although there may be slight differences between the customer (the household) and the user (the individual), the company can market directly to the individual representing the household or directly to the user. This also allows the company to match purchase behavior—when the customer made their first purchase, the level of purchases made in the past, and the number, type, and severity of service incidents— to that individual. With this information, the marketer can deliver highly targeted messages to that individual to reduce attrition and increase upsell and cross-sell.

Sophisticates

Most major companies with reasonable budgets ranging in the millions have embarked on modeling to inform their sales and marketing decision-making. They have reached a level of sophistication where modeling is *de rigueur*. They incorporate a level of market research, simple or complex attribution modeling, marketing mix modeling, and sales modeling across the larger units of their organizations. At least 80%, if not 90%, of their media budgets are modeled with a reasonable level of accuracy. The marketing team continues to seek out new data sources to model more and more of their media budget. Where applicable, they have implemented or are implementing:

- predictive modeling for their one-to-one customer relationships to mitigate churn and increase upselling and cross-selling;
- attribution modeling to improve their online presence;
- marketing mix modeling to optimize their acquisition activities;
- advanced modeling to improve their new product launches;
- and sales modeling to optimize their sales training, management, and execution.

The company has shifted from a focus on the sales function to a focus on the fully integrated sales and marketing functions.

With these modeling methods in place as the descriptive and predictive underpinnings of their sales and marketing decision-making, they now need to begin incorporating these models into a comprehensive rolling planning process to fully integrate their corporate vision with their strategic planning, their annual planning, and their tactical execution.

Most major advertisers are executing some or all of these sophisticated marketing modeling and ROI functions. Most companies with budgets in the millions have embarked either partially or fully on the appropriate modeling and analytic methods depending on whether they are B2B, B2C, sell to mass markets, or sell directly to individual consumers using one-to-one marketing.

Master marketing mechanics

There are currently only a handful of organizations achieving this level in the marketing machine continuum. These companies have medium to large marketing budgets ranging above $1 million per year and have determined that marketing execution excellence is just as valuable as great creative and excellent products in generating extraordinary results in competitive markets. These companies have fully integrated sophisticated modeling into their corporate vision and strategic and annual planning, as well as their tactical execution. They update their marketing decision-making through a regular monthly or weekly rolling planning process and workflow. They scrutinize new competitive and consumer insights through advanced simulation and scenario planning. Improving marketing ROI and constantly seeking the most effective media channels and propitious data sets are all part of their marketing prowess. They ceaselessly seek to run experiments in order to gain highly prized insights into consumer behavior. Old Amsterdam is a great example of a company that resides in this space. (See case study on Cheese That Goes Ka-Ching, pages 16-17.)

Marketers at this level must take extreme care to keep their proprietary methodologies for implementing the marketing machine in house. The design of their marketing machine is a critical pillar of their competitive advantage in the marketplace.

Chapter 4

What Can You Do With a Fully Functional Marketing Machine?

A marketing machine contributes enormous benefit to the organization. Predictability, certainty, and accountability in revenue generation is always better than the alternative. With a marketing machine, the organization can chart its growth and attract significantly higher levels of investment. Investors are always interested in low-risk, high-return investments. If the company can illustrate how marketing can deliver predictable and accountable revenue in proportion to an investment, then it will have higher value than an investment of similar size where the marketing investment is neither predictable nor accountable. Although ROI is at the heart of the marketing machine, it has much more value beyond providing sales achievement certainty.

What is a fully functioning marketing machine?

A marketing machine delivers high value, mostly through its certainty and predictability. Once these are in place, the company can now predict its costs to generate sales. The marketing machine translates marketing investments into certain expectations of sales revenue and volume. Although there is always some risk and uncertainty when looking into the future, these questions can be determined and entered into the equation. With certainty in the execution of the marketing plan, the marketing team can better plan and execute; longer term contracts and volume commitments can be made with confidence when negotiating media.

The marketing machine translates investments in marketing into direct revenue expectations. If the shareholders want to achieve a certain revenue target, the budgeting process can immediately determine the level of marketing budget required. With that uncertainty removed from the process, the rest of the company can now plan their budgets accordingly.

Improved operations

A marketing machine can provide further savings throughout the organization. With sales achievement certainty, manufacturing can plan better, build to capacity better, and make sure utilization rates are maximized.

With a marketing machine, the desired level of volume growth can be predicted. Workforce can be predicted. Over– or under-capacity situations are eliminated. If a new plant is required, the marketing machine can make certain that the plant build-out and available capacity are sold as soon as the plant comes online.

Knowing with certainty the level of sales can lead to enormous savings in the improved finished goods, work-in-process inventory levels, inventory carrying costs, purchasing volumes, production planning, and workforce planning. It can provide true streamlining of the organization. The marketing plan can now be confidently connected to the enterprise resource planning (ERP) system.

Dialing up the level of sales volume

Corporate growth can now be throttled up based on the management's capacity to handle and manage the growth and the level of investment required. Sales volume is now delivered based on a certain formula for marketing investment and sales achievement.

Personnel turnover

With a marketing machine in place, the management team can be very confident of the compensation plans that they negotiate, because they know the level of risk they are taking on with the proposed business and marketing plans. Job loss due to lack of achievement will be less of a risk. *The CMO tenure will be significantly longer.* The company will also have less turnover, leading to higher returns simply due to personnel stability.

Higher market shares

Although competitors may spend more, the company will be able to grow at a speed dialed in by the management team and the investors. This confidence in investment will lead to lower risk and therefore a higher willingness to invest more to grow market share faster. It doesn't necessarily mean that they will grow faster than the competition, but if the investors and management team are aggressive in their approach to the market, they *will* be able to dial-up faster growth.

Corporate budgeting

The budgeting process is now simplified, because the marketing budget can set the desired level of sales. The fallacious bargaining and haggling that now takes place between investments in marketing and investments in other areas of the company can now be eliminated because true trade-offs can be made between growth and operations/infrastructure.

The marketing machine and diminishing returns

Investors, businesses, and marketers unfortunately can't invest unlimited funds into a marketing machine and obtain unlimited outputs. The law of diminishing returns is always at work, and it means that as the company dials up the marketing investments, less and less revenue becomes available for each incremental unit of marketing investment.

To determine the best level of short-term and long-term investment, the diminishing returns expectations of the marketing machine must be considered. There are many factors to consider.

Short term

Short-term diminishing returns limit the potential growth of the brand because the brand only has a certain level of connection with the consumer. If too much growth is expected in the short term, the diminishing returns curve bends more quickly. There simply aren't enough connections to enough consumers to drive extensive short-term growth. Diminishing returns exhibits a sharper curve, soon limiting the incremental returns a brand can expect for each incremental investment in marketing.

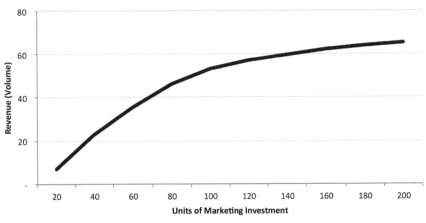

Figure 4: Diminishing Returns

Long-term

In a relatively stable industry, as new customers are won, market share increases, and the brand expands in the population, the diminishing returns curve moves up and flattens. In the long term, the brand can leverage short-term investments to drive long-term growth and a flatter diminishing returns curve.

Category or industry segment growth

Industry segment growth also tends to de-sharpen the diminishing returns curve. As more consumers enter the category, the diminishing returns curve becomes less sharp, because the media investment per target consumer doesn't saturate. In a constrained category, the media investment is spread over the same number of consumers. In a growing category where new consumers are entering the industry segment, more media is required to reach these new entrants. This tends to flatten the diminishing returns curve.

Investment goods v. consumables

Long-lived investment products have different diminishing returns curves than those of consumables. Certain consumables also have different responses to advertising. In many consumables categories, such as salty snacks or chocolates, the level of advertising tends to increase the category size. The more advertising people see, the more they purchase of these types of products. With more of these products in the pantry, consumption increases. Advertising tends to grow the category size in the short term.

On the other hand, investment goods tend to have a fixed demand. Once the market is saturated, no more new-product purchases are required. Only replacement purchases need to be made. Advertising can have a slight impact on pulling purchases forward for those units that are faulty and have exhibited high ongoing repair costs, but this effect is much, much smaller than with consumables. For example, a homeowner isn't going to replace their furnace just because they saw an ad. However, when the furnace is close to the end of its life and has already been repaired many times, then it is possible that advertising combined with an offer could pull the replacement furnace purchase forward.

The single source of truth

For example, different groups within the same global company may use different, non-homogeneous sources for their version of the truth. In smaller, less developed countries, where accurate sell-through data isn't available, they may only be able to report sell-in. In larger, more advanced countries where sell-through data is available, they may report both sell-in and sell-through. Similarly, in larger countries where they can afford monthly brand tracking studies, they may be able to report brand health metrics on a monthly basis; where in smaller countries, they may only be able to report them quarterly or annually. The company needs a single source of truth such that the numbers can be consistent from one country to the next, one product to the next, and one distribution channel to the next. This is not an easy task, but it is getting easier. For major multi-nationals with the same metrics orthodoxy around the world, the company needs a single picture of its ability to have achieved the numbers in the past and its ability to achieve the numbers in the future. The numbers must also easily blend forward and back so that they are seamless across time horizons.

CEOs need one source of truth (using the same definition of "truth"), regardless of whether it is measuring shipments from the past or sell-through into the future. In smaller organizations, they may not know to directly ask for this single source of truth, but it is critical to properly manage the business. This marketing accounting enables the company to truly know what's going on in the organization with a consistent measuring stick. Although financial tracking requires that shipments into the sales channel be measured with stringent recordkeeping, what is more important for an understanding of company success is the level of consumption *at the point of consumption,* i.e., with the consumer.

Although the sales team is often responsible for shipping products from the factory doors, marketing owns both the future and what is sold through to the consumer, i.e., what gets pulled off the shelves. It owns the measurement method and definition of what happens at the point of consumption, because what matters is what the consumer purchased, what they have in the pantry or in their internal stocks, and what they consume and when they consume it. In many cases consumption is equated with sell-through (what is purchased in the store), but it is also important to understand the level of inventory the consumer has stored in their pantries, in their vanity drawers, and in their garages. Although marketers often focus on what was sold in the store, if the items are stored in the pantry or in the garage, the marketer may need to continue their marketing to make certain that the items get consumed so as not to hinder the next sale.

Section Two:
Marketing Needs to Be Agile

Chapter 5

What Is Marketing Agility?

The objective for any business is to deliver consistent financial results that meet or exceed expectations. Delivering under expectations is akin to failure. If it happens very often then heads will roll, at the top and the bottom of the organization. No organization can survive without growth unless it can consistently make a profit or meet or exceed expectations. No organization can be successful in the market unless it can deliver financial results that outpace other investments in terms of returns for a given level of risk. If we define risk as uncertainty, then a company that can deliver results that are more certain and continue to provide dividends on a consistent basis is more valuable compared with other investments that may be more uncertain.

On the other hand, no one can predict the future. Twenty years ago, no one would have guessed that an upstart social media platform named Facebook would have more users than the population of the largest country on earth. No one would have guessed that mobile technology would be the most popular method to access the Internet. No one would have guessed that Apple would have been the most valuable company in the world[10] and that it would be able to pack more computing power into a handheld device than what was used to land a man on the moon. The future is inherently unpredictable, and predictability seems to be diminishing. It is unusually unusual. The weather patterns seem more intense, political upheaval seems to be more rampant, and the impact of these factors on local markets seems more extreme.

An unpredictable future and a desire for certainty are at odds, and marketers must do their best to drive sales for the organization in a way that

---

[10] https://www.forbes.com/sites/kurtbadenhausen/2017/05/23/apple-heads-the-worlds-most-valuable-brands-of-2017-at-170-billion/#24f64fee384b, August 27, 2017

provides what the investors want against the uncertainties in the market. The best way to be successful in an uncertain world is to be agile. To be able to react to dynamics in the marketplace with a relatively short lead time.

Dynamics in the marketplace can be either positive or negative. Competitors act in their own self-interest and make successful new thrusts to disrupt the market. Or, competitors make mistakes and marketers need to capitalize on them. External factors can reduce or increase demand. Gas prices go down and consumers have more disposable income; gas prices go up and consumers have less disposable income. Channel partners overextend themselves and need to pull back. Sales channels move online and offer access to new customers, but at lower overall margins. Smart marketers act in the marketplace and learn to understand the early warning signs of impending changes in dynamics and, with agility, they make better decisions and react in time to achieve the expected financial results—consistently and on time. In the following section are a few example disruptions that marketers need to react to with agility in order to provide investors and the CEO a more certain expectation of planned and projected financial results.

Successful, new competitive product/brand launch

A successful competitive launch can have devastating impact on a few and possibly all competitors in the market. If the market has only a few competitors, the impact will most likely be larger and have some impact on all competitors, but more impact on some than others. The agile marketer must quickly determine the expected impact on their share in the marketplace in the face of this launch. They must determine whether the new product will grow the category and raise all boats or decrease sales as the new product grows and takes market share. If the category has a lot of competitors, then the impact on each of the competitors may be relatively small. If the new product delivers new capabilities, then the overall category size may grow. Nevertheless, marketers must constantly be ready to respond to any new competitive launch. They need to be able to have at the ready a response plan that they can implement if and when the situation arises. If not, they may need to significantly overspend and sacrifice profit at a later date to deliver the required sales. Marketers need agility to see the potential threat and be ready to respond at an optimal level in order to not significantly adversely affect expected profitability.

Unsuccessful, new competitive product/launch

Most new product launches fail. According to most sources, 75% of new consumer packaged goods launches fail to achieve $7.5m in revenue in the first year. Only 3% achieve over $50m in first year revenue.[11] IRI publishes an annual New Product Pacesetters Report and found that in 2015, over 10,000 new products were introduced, with only 10 achieving over $100m in first year sales. "An estimated 90 percent fail to achieve the milestones set before them."[12] Marketers must take care not to overreact and waste precious, limited marketing resources fretting over a new competitive product introduction that will have limited impact on the market.

Channel disruption

With the advent of e-commerce and online sales, many brick-and-mortar retailers are being forced to shutter their stores in favor of building out sophisticated online e-commerce sites. In China, social platforms and internet service providers have been very creative in building out online shopping platforms that smooth the online payment and deliver the goods the same day for many of the major cities. WeChat allows payment directly in the application. Taobao, a Chinese online shopping website founded by the Alibaba Group, built out its Taobao marketplace, T-Mall, to offer brands an ability to build an online store. In 2015, Alibaba is now bigger than Amazon and eBay combined. Alibaba managed to achieve $5.75bn in sales on Black Friday, larger than all US e-commerce sites combined across both Thanksgiving and Black Friday.[13]

With these shifts in consumer purchase behavior, traditional brick-and-mortar relationships with manufacturers are being strained, providing competitors in all categories new opportunities to disrupt the market.

In the U.S., Amazon is king, but Walmart and Target are quickly building out their online stores to compete while they (and others, such as Macy's, Best Buy and JC Penney) shutter their brick-and-mortar stores. In 2016,

---

[11] https://hbr.org/2011/04/why-most-product-launches-fail, October 2016.
[12] http://www.iriworldwide.com/IRI/media/IRI-New-Product-Pacesetters-Report-April2016.pdf, October 2016.
[13] http://www.theverge.com/2014/5/7/5690596/meet-alibaba-the-ecommerce-giant-with-more-sales-than-amazon-and-ebay, October 2016.

Macy's closed 36 stores, Best Buy 50 stores,[14] and Kmart/Sears 78 stores.[15],[16] Even Walmart will close 269 stores, while they acquire jet.com, the online retailer, to compete with the ever-growing juggernaut of e-commerce.

Successful marketing campaigns

The Aflac duck "Park Bench" commercial (created by the Kaplan-Thaler advertising agency) was initially launched in January of 2000.[17] Nobody could have foreseen how this one creative concept would transform the supplemental insurance industry. The campaign was so successful that the duck was incorporated into the company's logo. This single campaign was

---

[14] http://www.cbsnews.com/news/best-buys-store-closing-list-is-yours-on-it/, October 2016.

[15] http://www.usatoday.com/story/money/business/2016/08/11/retailers-closing-stores-macys-walmart-kmart-sears-aeropostale/88560318/, October 2016.

[16] http://investorplace.com/2016/01/macys-store-closing-list-m/#.V8sOL2Uz1eE, October 2016.

[17] https://www.Aflac.com/about-Aflac/our-company/the-Aflac-duck.aspx, October 2016.

instrumental in growing the supplemental insurance industry and stealing share from its nearest competitors. The company now enjoys a very high level of brand awareness in the marketplace. Marketers on both sides of a campaign launch need to be constantly tracking critical interim brand metrics in order to be prepared for a new marketing campaign's success and—if you're unlucky enough to be their competitor—to know how to react against it in order to mitigate potential volume losses.

Company new product launch and competitive responses

A product launch is one of the riskiest career events for any marketer. Successful launches can catapult a career. Unsuccessful launches can ruin it. Successful launches are driven by the right balance of distribution, pricing, advertising, and consumer trialing. If there isn't enough product on the shelf when the advertising begins, demand has just been created for the competition. If the level of distribution is too high for the level of demand, the retailers will want to reallocate their shelf space to other, more productive, brands. Worse yet, they may never want to invest their valuable shelf space in that brand or product again. If the advertising doesn't build initial consumer trial, the product will waste away on the shelf. If the value and experience of the new product underwhelms the first trialers, they will not repurchase. If consumers can't be made to change their habitual brand purchase to try the new product, the product will fail. Marketers must monitor this process on a very short time cycle in order to make certain that, as the product rolls out, it meets (and hopefully beats) expectations.

Marketers must also worry about competitive response to their brand launch. If immediately prior to the launch the competition tries to load the consumer's pantries with their existing substitute product, this defensive action will delay the impact of the first consumer trial, thereby slowing the initial trial and reducing initial growth rates. Competitors can also launch new products that compete directly with the new features and benefits offered, so that they, too, will benefit as consumers learn to value the new product and its new feature set. Especially in the technology space, competitors can be expected to leapfrog your product offering with a superior feature set in order to bring to market a new product that surpasses the benefits offered in your initial technology leap.

Case Study: Singles Day

External factors can have a major effect on marketing tactics. On November 11, 2009, in China, Alibaba launched a new sales event for the traditional "Singles' Day," symbolized by the four lonely ones of "11/11." It was even further enhanced in 2011 when the date read 11/11/11.[2] In the past, it was Chinese tradition that on November 11th single men would lament their unmarried status with a drink, but Jack Ma, founder of Alibaba, seized the opportunity to launch this new one-day sales event. Although the event was characterized by one-time only promotional prices, the event has morphed into the largest single-day online shopping event in the world, surging to sales worth $14.3bn in 2015—a 60% increase over the prior year. Sales volumes exceed those of Black Friday holiday shopping in the U.S.

This holiday does generate increased sales, but it does so at high cost. Competition is so high on Singles' Day that price promotions cut deeply into profits. The question for marketers is whether the sales made on this day cannibalize sales that would have otherwise taken place either before or after the sales event. Did they simply shift volume to the Singles' Day promotion by shoppers wanting to take advantage of the lower prices on items they would have otherwise purchased at full price? Marketers need analytics in order to know how much inventory to make available for sale at the lower price. They need to know the level of cannibalized sales that could have otherwise occurred at full price. They need to know whether new customers were reached at this promotional price that would have otherwise not purchased from the company. And they need to know whether higher volumes were achieved that otherwise would not have materialized from their existing customers due to the lower prices.

[1] http://www.reuters.com/article/us-alibaba-singles-day-idUSKCN0SZ34J20151111, October 2016.
[2] http://www.nytimes.com/2013/11/12/business/international/online-shopping-marathon-zooms-off-the-blocks-in-china.html?_r=0, October 2016.

External factors

External factors can influence the entire category, a few brands in the category, or a single brand. The French wine boycott in 1996[18] in Britain due to the French protest against British nuclear tests led to a decrease in imports of French wine by over 30%. Other non-French wine brands were able to garner the demand created by this boycott. This external factor had a negative impact on one group of vintners and helped another.

---

[18] http://www.independent.co.uk/news/french-wine-boycott-successful-1317133.html.

As shown in the examples above, disruption can come from any angle; marketers need to be prepared and ready to accurately build responses into their plans in an agile manner.

To be agile, marketers need to take these steps:

1. See what's coming over the horizon.
2. Plan for agility.
3. Remember time is of the essence.
4. Focus on scenario building.
5. Accept the no-win situation.

See what's coming over the horizon

Seeing what's coming over the horizon is the most important activity for the savvy marketer. CEOs must provide their input on these trends to make certain that they are not under- or over-emphasized. If the trends aren't foreseen, they can't and won't be planned for—then if and when they take place, it may be too late.

Trends

Some trends are just that and can be easily forecast. For example, many market research services predict that e-commerce is expected to grow at about 15% per year for the next 3 years.[19] This is a trend that can be incorporated relatively easily into the marketers' model. Smart marketers already include these kinds of trends in their forecast models. In addition, they may also test the sensitivity of their plans to a growth rate of 10% or 20% in order to determine any hidden barriers or potential opportunities to be ready for.

Seasonality

Some trends only have an impact during certain times of the year. Christmas is at the same time every year, and for the most part, Christmas shopping

---

[19] http://www.emarketer.com/Article/Global-B2C-Ecommerce-Sales-Hit-15-Trillion-This-Year-Driven-by-Growth-Emerging-Markets/1010575, October 2016.

begins on Black Friday after Thanksgiving and continues through New Year's Day with post-Christmas sales, returns and exchanges. For example, summer is the high season for beverage sales and during this period, beverage advertising is more effective. Similarly, sunscreen advertising will be more effective immediately before and during the summer than other times of the year.

The 2010 FIFA World Cup in South Africa and beer sales in Malaysia

In 2010, when the World Cup took place in South Africa, it had an interesting impact on sales of beer in Southeast Asia over 5,000 miles away. Malaysia has a large, growing youth population very interested in international soccer. During the World Cup, beer sales in Malaysia were up an inordinate amount. The reason: the 6-hour time difference between South Africa and Malaysia meant the broadcasting of the live games took place late in the evening in Malaysia. This meant that the bars would be open longer and would be more filled with soccer fans enjoying the hoppy brew than would otherwise be the case, for example, if they were played in a different time zone in South America or in Japan.

Some trends are multi-year and are therefore more difficult to capture. In the U.S., the presidential elections occur on a four-year cycle; publishers can expect their sales of ad space to skyrocket during the lead-up to the quadrennial elections. Similarly, the FIFA World Cup is on a four-year cycle (see case study above).

Some trends are seasonal but shift in periodicity. Ramadan is the most important holiday in countries with large Muslim populations. This holiday moves on the basis of a lunar calendar; thus it takes place at a different time every year. When this overlaps with other, fixed holidays, planning needs to take this into consideration to make certain the impact of both holidays is properly forecasted.

Stochastic

Some external factors are stochastic or random, but take place nevertheless. These are typically due to the weather. No one knows when it will rain, but rain it will. Most weather-related events simply shift demand forward or back. Only when the weather impacts, for example, a major travel holiday such as Labor Day, will sales potentially be permanently impacted for the season and possibly the year. Depending on the market, since the demand may be impacted generally, marketers may need to include a probabilistic estimate into their forecasts.

On the other hand, no one knows when a hurricane or tornado will hit or the level of devastation it will wreak. If the damage is massive and long term, marketers may then need to make adjustments, typically in the local region, to account for the impact on product sales. This impact can also be estimated probabilistically to factor in a level of uncertainty in the planning for these stochastic events. For companies prone to these types of disruptions, such as those with large markets in the coastal areas of Texas, Florida, Mississippi, and Louisiana, any storm's impact must be tracked so that it can be used for risk estimation in the future.

Own marketing actions

During every planning cycle, marketers try to come up with ways to grow their share in the market. Some of those plans are relatively static, others are highly disruptive. In either case, marketers aim to build integrated marketing plans that coordinate pricing and distribution with promotions and new product launches (or discontinuations). Because it may not be possible to execute a plan exactly as planned, marketers must be ready to continually readjust their plans to achieve the best outcomes. In election years, the price of media may soar or commercial slots may not be available. In distribution, from year to year the level of product display space may not be available, or it may not be possible to achieve the level of shelf space originally projected. For a small business, the company may not be able to get the inventory financing in the time frame expected. On the positive side, media channels may sometimes be able to offer additional options available at special rates that weren't initially available when the marketing plan was built. Or, a sponsorship opportunity to name an NFL stadium may suddenly appear. Agile marketers need to be able to quickly incorporate these opportunities and challenges into their thinking and determine what the best option is, given their expectation of the impact of these opportunities and challenges.

This is something that shouldn't be done on the fly and shouldn't be done shooting from the hip. It should be done through a concerted effort with a planning process in place that allows the marketer to easily update their plans, test the new scenarios, and quickly make decisions. It requires a continuous, rolling planning cycle that, depending on the dynamics in the industry segment, should be done on a monthly, weekly, or even daily basis. This will allow the agile marketer a formal opportunity to quickly assess upcoming trends and unplanned events so they can react as quickly and as accurately as possible.

Competitive disruptive actions

Just as we develop marketing plans that try to be disruptive, so too, do our competitors. The Aflac duck campaign and some new product launches, such as Dannon's Oikos Triple Zero Greek yogurt, are great examples of competitive disruptions. Tracking and estimating the potential impact of these disruptions is critical to salvaging the sales of an existing product/brand. If there is information available prior to the actual launch, the potential impact of the launch can be projected and the response can be optimized. Once the launch takes place, if it has been foreseen and the marketing team has already done its marketing plan stress testing, then marketing will be ready with potential response packages, hastening the implementation and approval process to get the response into action as quickly as possible.

With an understanding of what's coming over the horizon, marketers can now develop expectations of the future. With a strong internally developed focus on potential disruptions in the marketplace, marketers can more easily and more quickly build disruptions into their response planning. Agile marketers must gather market insights about potential threats from many sources and disseminate them into what is real, what may be real, and what is erroneous. By combining these insights with their best expectations of known trends in the marketplace, marketers can build a finely tuned expectation of the future.

Plan for agility

Agility doesn't take place just because we will it to be so. We need to plan for it. The best plans have the largest amount of options available for the widest range of decisions at the last possible moment.

There is a cost to being able to have these options available and it has several primary components:

1. The option to rapidly purchase media
2. The ability to quickly update the creative concept
3. The management ability to make the decision
4. The staffing to carry out a modified marketing plan
5. The time to regularly review the current state of affairs and possible future states of affairs

In an ideal world, we would be able to make a creative change within a few short minutes and get it on air within seconds. But we know this is unrealistic when we have legal review requirements and potential regulatory review requirements (e.g., the Office of Prescription Drug Promotion in pharmaceuticals in the U.S.). Regulatory or legal approval time lags affect the speed with which the creative component of the advertising can be modified and determines the minimum organizational reaction times. If the planning cycle is on a weekly basis, the fastest the team may be able to react is within a week. If an initial deviation can be seen after one week, but is not determined to be a trend until 3 weeks later, then the reaction time of the marketing planning team is a minimum of 3 weeks. If TV ad-buying is typically 4 weeks out for non-spot, then there is a 4-week lag time. All of these lags add up to slow reactions to potential disruptions in the market. By continuously monitoring the market, agile marketers can reduce the lag times and make significantly better, faster, and more certain decisions.

All of these factors play a strong role in the actual ability of an organization to respond to competitive threats, external factors, or even unsuccessful media creatives. Knowing these time lag effects ahead of time can help determine the level of agility available in the system in order to build workflows and internal processes to mitigate organizational delays in response.

Remember time is of the essence.[20]

We all know that time marches ever forward, that foreseeing and recognizing a market dynamic this week is better than recognizing it one week later. It is critical to be prepared for a potential disruption and to have fully researched options available.

Many times, a disruption isn't immediately clear. An outlier may be discovered, but determining whether it is a trend, a major disruption, or a simple anomaly may take more than one planning cycle. There are two types of outliers:

1. Certain one-time outliers (anomalies) – With some outliers, the reasons can be quickly determined, planning can begin, and corrective action can be immediately taken. It could be a new competitive ad campaign, a new product launch, or a major storm. With very little investigatory work, these can be quickly identified and dealt with.
2. Potential trends – With other outliers, it may be several planning cycles before a trend has been verified or it can be determined with confidence to be a one-time anomaly. Once the outlier is identified as a trend, pre-defined corrective actions can be quickly executed.

Even before the reasons for the outlier are known with full certainty, the outlier can still be acted upon. Granted, the response actions may be less than optimal; however, in most cases, it is better to have begun remedial action earlier rather than later. If remedial actions are not taken early enough, the cost of a major correction can be prohibitive. Thus acting sub-optimally in the short term is in most cases better than not acting and potentially falling into a greater sales abyss by acting much later.

Even if marketing overcompensates by dipping into the marketing reserve, at some later date after the pressure is off, there will be room to make a slight planned cutback to regain partially or wholly the marketing reserve.

---

[20] http://www.forbes.com/sites/forbesagencycouncil/2016/09/08/for-modern-marketers-time-is-money/#720090a33efc, October 2016.

Focus on scenario building.

No marketer can fully determine what is going to happen in the future. Nevertheless, agile marketers can learn from the future by looking at what might happen and developing specific scenarios against which they can optimize their marketing plans. They can also look at the risks associated with each of these futures in order to build a plan that incorporates these risks and provides the ability to swiftly reroute marketing resources once a particular scenario is ruled in or ruled out. In addition, as scenarios unfold, new scenarios may develop against which the agile marketer needs to build new plans, requiring further optimization and detailed risk assessment.

Accept the no-win situation.

Sometimes a situation is so bad (for example, a product recall) that even further investments in marketing will not allow a full recovery. Nevertheless, it is incumbent on the marketing team to make certain that the losses resulting from these revenue disruptions are as low as possible. (For example, see the Volkswagen diesel engine emission scandal on page 100.) Having a marketing machine in place for all products and their sister product lines helps to quickly minimize the tide of losses with certainty and predictability. Without it, an organization would have to make less-than-certain estimates as to how to respond. Businesses could potentially lose many weeks, if not months, in developing a remediation strategy for the sister products as well as for the problem- and scandal-plagued products themselves.

Marketers own the future by predicting, modeling, and preparing thoroughly. By keeping multiple scenarios in mind and prioritizing speed and response time marketers can begin to move with agility through unexpected hurdles. The key is to expect that hurdles, in some form, will inevitably occur. To be consistently agile, however, certain recurring activities and actions must be worked into the planning cycles. This allows the marketing machine to run smoothly and almost automatically with minimal redirection from the team.

Chapter 6

What Makes Marketers Agile?

There are seven critical components to agile marketing.

1. A regular planning process
2. Marketing plan stress testing
3. Standardized response packages
4. Continuous rolling planning
5. Putting boundaries on the unknown knowns and unknown unknowns
6. The marketing reserve
7. Owning the future

A regular planning process

Most companies do reasonably well at building an annual plan. With fiscal years often ending with the calendar year, the annual corporate planning process begins about 6 months in advance, usually in the summer. This process defines the budgets necessary to achieve the functions and activities expected to be in place for the next year. There are compromises between the sales and revenue expectations and the operations to be able to build and maintain capacity to meet the forecasted demand at the desired profit. There are negotiations between the shareholders and the executive team to deliver more profit and higher revenue without further investment to keep the stock price growing. There are negotiations between the sales team and the marketing team to align marketing investments in demand-generation with the expected sales resources to fulfill that demand.

Making the CMO truly accountable

The tenure of a typical CMO hovers around the 24-month mark. Some years it's better, some worse. A fully implemented marketing machine can help to increase the CMO's tenure as it becomes clear that the execution is properly in place and that the root cause of market disruptions can be quickly identified. If the cause is from forces external to the company, the marketer can point out that they were properly identified on time and had corrective actions quickly in place. If the lackluster sales are assumed to be due to internal execution, then it is the CMO who is solely responsible. With a marketing machine the CMO is now back in control of his/her destiny.

It's easy to recognize a non-marketing machine company. If marketing isn't considered a revenue machine, the marketing budget is often set as a simple percentage of sales, a simple percentage of profit, or some other number based on industry benchmarks researched and pushed by the CFO. Worse yet, if marketing is considered an expense, it will simply be cut at the first sign of lackluster results.

Misalignment of marketing and sales with company projections can take place in several ways:

1. First, especially for small businesses and B2B marketers, businesses fail to consider the lag time between marketing actions and the first revenue generated from those actions. For example, let's assume a company has an average sales cycle of 6 months once a qualified lead has been generated. If marketing is able to generate 100 high quality leads in January, the expected revenue will not be realized until July. Sales has a 6-month lag between the initial marketing activity and its ability to generate conversions. However, long sales cycle marketing planning rarely accounts for this lag in their planning processes. If corporate planning begins in July for a January fiscal year start, for marketing to have any impact on sales in January, it needs to begin *executing* its marketing plan in July. Its own fiscal planning needs to have begun months earlier. This means that for marketing to be in sync with corporate execution, marketing *execution* needs to begin in July in order for the resulting sales to take effect in the first month of the corporate plan in January!

Thus the marketing plan needs to begin execution just as the corporate planning process is beginning. Unfortunately, few if any companies build this lag into their planning process. This means that because marketing actions for the new year only begin in January, they will have no impact until July. This is a disastrous situation and one that leads directly to short tenures in the senior marketing team. Because marketing actions taken in January were un-impactful on sales for January and the first quarter, the business is obliged to cut marketing because in their minds, *it's not working!* It didn't deliver any sales in January, so why are we wasting money on marketing?

But the situation gets worse. Because the marketing budget is now cut—quite often for the rest of the year—marketing for January in the next year is also seen as ineffective because there was no marketing in the prior July. This is a never-ending death spiral for many businesses with long sales cycles.

Planning for a 5-year sales cycle

Businesses with sales cycles lasting many years face interesting challenges. For example, companies that sell chemicals often have long multi-year sales cycles. Here is an example:

1. First the new chemical is invented.
2. Next marketing must generate leads so that engineers can evaluate the chemical for their use. The evaluation process may take months to years, depending on the priorities of the prospective customer and their ability to build it into their existing or new product designs.
3. Once the evaluation is complete, the prospect can then begin building a manufacturing capability to make their new product using the new chemical. In some cases, this can easily last over a year.
4. Then once the manufacturing facility is built, the customer needs to begin selling the product and hopefully they can reach their revenue expectations.
5. This also doesn't happen overnight.

By the time the chemical has reached its expected volumes it could be years after the initial marketing activity was executed. Designing a marketing machine for these types of long lead sales cycles requires a tracking mechanism that tracks success at each point along the entire sales process.

---

2. Marketing response for small, medium, and even some large businesses is often lumpy. For example, for high-tech B2B companies, most marketing leads are generated from a large annual national or international trade show. There is only one trade show during the year, but the exposure to actual prospective buyers is enormous. Many times, the number of high-quality leads may overwhelm the capacity of the sales team. This means that some leads may actually be lost because it wasn't possible to properly follow up on them in a timely fashion. The company simply didn't have the necessary bandwidth in sales or marketing due to the high-level spike of leads generated from this single trade show event.

3. Marketing generates a mix of high-, medium-, and low-quality leads. In an ideal world, marketing would generate only top-quality leads that convert quickly with a high probability at a high value with a minimum of conversion cost. Unfortunately, just about every marketing program also generates leads that may not convert, may convert for a low value, or may only convert with significant conversion costs. Marketing planning must take this into account in order to build the right process to hand over primarily top-quality leads to the expensive sales team. Marketing then needs to keep low-quality leads in marketing so they can be nurtured until they are ready to be converted by the higher cost sales team.

Marketing plan stress-testing

Before a marketing plan can be built and approved, it needs to be stress-tested. Marketing plans are generated with certain expectations of the future. As discussed previously, these expectations need to include assumptions about internal execution challenges, competitive actions, channel actions, and external factors. Stress-testing the plan provides the marketer and the CEO justification for certain levels of acceptable risk.

For the CEO

Companies must match their cost of messaging with the value those messages produce. There are 3 tiers of messaging costs: the outside sales team, the inside sales team, and the marketing team.

The Outside Sales Team is generally the most expensive per message per prospective customer. The outside sales team is generally made up of the best sales professionals. Not only does the company need to pay their base salaries and their commissions, but they also need to factor in their travel and other expenses of meeting face-to-face with prospective customers.

The Inside Sales Team is less expensive per message per prospective customer because they don't travel and are usually dividing their time working across many prospective customers.

The Marketing Team and associated working media costs are the least expensive per message per customer because they are generally not working on a one-to-one basis. Instead they are sending out many messages through a variety of different media channels to many, many prospective customers.

For example, if unemployment is higher than expected and it requires an extra $2 million in the marketing budget to overcome this scenario, where will this extra investment come from? Will it come out of profit, or will it come out of some other corporate function? If the launch was significantly more successful than expected, where will the cash come from to finance the increased inventory? The marketing plan under each of these scenarios needs to be stress-tested in order to understand the risks and plan contingencies accordingly. The uncertainties in projecting the future across highly influential external variables will determine the potential sources of investment. Depending on the sources and levels of uncertainty, the executive team will need to determine whether the money needs to be set aside from other investment sources or made available through the marketing reserve as described below.

The marketing reserve

Marketers need to react quickly in order to capitalize on revenue opportunities, as well as adjust when they see that their plans aren't going to achieve expectations. A marketing reserve can facilitate this speedy reaction by quickly providing extra funds when they are needed. In order to make this work, the initial marketing budget needs to be set to achieve the corporate plan based on the expectations of the future and the associated risk thereof. This is the base level of marketing investment required, given the foreseen scenarios of internal execution challenges, competitive threats, and channel and external factors. The marketing reserve is then calculated as an additional 15% to 20% of the base level marketing plan; this is made available to the marketing team when the going gets tough or there are marketing strategies and tactics that are working significantly better than expected.

The marketing reserve and bad debt

The marketing reserve can be likened to a "bad debt reserve" in accounts receivable. Most companies expect that about 2% of their invoices won't be paid. A reserve is accrued throughout the year so that as a small percentage of invoices aren't paid, the loss can be expensed against this accrual. In that way, the company has a better estimate of what their true profit will be, without having a surprise write-off of uncollected invoices at the end of the year.

Standardized response packages

In marketing, there are a handful of highly likely scenarios that can take place. Each of them can be planned for and stress tested in order to make certain the best options have been chosen. These can be thought of as response packages. One package could be for an unexpected competitive new product introduction. One could be for the loss of a distribution channel partner. One could be for some unusual external factor, such as a major hurricane or some other natural event. Each of these response packages can be pre-tested so that the marketing team can learn from them and can quickly act on them, if and when it becomes necessary.

For example, one response package may be pre-defined in response to a potential competitive price drop or some other type of price promotion.

Although pricing responses may not be quickly executable, they can at least reduce any lag time in their planning. If these response packages have been pre-defined, they can be pre-tested and pre-optimized. Then, with the marketing machine in place, when the disruption occurs, the response package can be quickly adjusted for the exact requirements of the disruption, without needing multiple levels of laborious scenario testing and painful management approval. Rigorous testing won't be required, because the outlines of the plan will have already been pre-tested. The response packages are nearly ready out of the box. The sales and marketing team can begin implementing the response with a much shorter turnaround time.

Response packages and pizza dough

In most pizzerias dough is pre-made and put in the refrigerator for when it is needed during the busy lunch and dinner hours. Instead of having to make the pizza dough with every order, the laborious process of combining the ingredients and mixing and kneading are done ahead of time. In this way, the restaurant can quickly add the toppings and bake to order as soon as the pizza order is received. Similarly, response packages are pre-defined and pre-tested so that the marketer only needs to adjust the specifics of the package based on the particular details of the competitive, channel, or external action.

Continuous, rolling planning

In highly dynamic markets, opportunities can quickly arise and threats can quickly appear. Marketers must be in a position to take advantage of these opportunities and/or respond to these threats. Depending on the marketing environment, data availability, and other factors, a rolling planning process should take place on either a weekly or a monthly basis. We've often found that it is best to start with a monthly cycle, but then quickly move to a weekly cycle once the workflows have been established.

For almost every company, it is critical to make the quarterly fiscal numbers. As a result, we've found that a rolling planning cycle should plan forward at least 90 days or even 120 days into the future. In this way, the plan is always looking into the future so that the numbers for the quarter will be achieved. The monthly or weekly planning cycle needs to incorporate all the most recent data from sales, marketing, competition, and channel and external factors. Then it needs to run scenarios based on this data and optimize the 90-day rolling plan to meet the sales objectives for that 90 days. If it's determined early on that it's not possible to meet these objectives with the existing budget, the marketing reserve can be activated and invested as necessary to counteract any forecasted shortfall. In this way, if each 90-day plan corrects for forecasted shortfalls and the marketing plan is adjusted to meet these shortfalls, then the company can be nearly 100% certain that the marketing machine can achieve the fiscal quarterly sales and profit objectives, leading to expected stock price growth and reduced risk in the stock.

The known knowns

"There are known knowns. These are things we know that we know. There are known unknowns. That is to say, there are things that we know we don't know. But there are also unknown unknowns. There are things we don't know we don't know."[1]

Donald Rumsfeld

[1] http://www.brainyquote.com/quotes/quotes/d/donaldrums148142.html, October 2016.

The known knowns and the unknown unknowns

When putting together a strategic plan, an annual marketing plan, or a rolling marketing plan, there are always trends and events we can estimate with reasonable accuracy. At the other end of the spectrum are things we don't even know we don't know. Since we can never fully predict the future, we can only do our best to make predictions about what might happen and then let our model determine how best to act with those predictions in place. Different predictions or estimates of the future can be wrapped up into a scenario; the model can then provide accurate scenario planning to deliver the best options given the predictions built into the scenario.

Known knowns

When we look at the future there are the known knowns. We know we will launch a new product with an investment of $20 million in advertising. We know the national annual trade show will take place on October 20.

Known unknowns

There are the known unknowns. We know that if the competition launches a new product it will receive advertising support somewhere in the range between $10 million and $20 million, but the exact level is not known for certain. The organization can identify where missing information exists and, to a large extent, put bounds around the lack of information. In this case, the estimated competitive marketing plan is bounded by $10 million and $20 million. It is in these areas that marketers and the organization need to work very hard to gather as much information as possible, even if incomplete, to help fill the gaps. As time moves forward, the bounds get narrower and the gaps get smaller.

Unknown unknowns

There are the unknown unknowns. No one can predict catastrophic events, but being prepared can provide management the best information to make the best decisions when they occur. No one ever imagined the failure mode that doomed the fate of the Challenger space shuttle. The unknown unknowns are driven mostly by the failure to fully imagine prospective scenarios that might befall the project or the business.

In order to fully understand the impact of unknowns in the future, scenarios must be built that envision potential threats in order to understand their potential impact and develop plans or response packages to mitigate them. Although the exact scenario, by definition, can't be foreseen, at least an imagined scenario may be close and provide insight as to how this unforeseen event might impact the company and how the company should respond.

Unknown knowns

Many business managers question whether unknown knowns exist, but in large organizations there is organizational forgetfulness. People forget that they knew something, although when asked about something, they'll respond, "Yes, I do remember that." Or the knowledge may be in some other department and not readily available to everyone. Siloes in large organizations tend to hoard their information, making it difficult to disseminate across the organization. In other instances, the answers may be believed to be known, but need to be reverified.

For the CEO

The marketer predicts, the model projects.

Predictions and projections

When it comes to making plans for the future and stress-testing those plans, marketers must make estimates of what they see as future trends and future possibilities. These predictions about possible futures are the responsibility of the marketer. The marketer owns the future and that future is made up of a set of predictions. Various combinations of these predictions make up a scenario: a collection of a specific set of predictions against which a marketing machine, a model, can make projections. The role of the model is not to make predictions. The role of the model is to make projections of the future given a certain set of predictions defined by a specific scenario.

Aligning the strategic plan with the annual plan with the monthly or weekly rolling plan

The strategic plan

Strategic plans generally look a handful of years or possibly many years into the future. They can encompass the launch of a product, its growth, the mature phase, and possibly its demise. The idea is that investors invest in the product because they see some opportunity for a healthy return on that investment. They expect that there will be initial years where the business will be cash-flow negative, but at some point, the business will be cash-flow positive and pay dividends to the original investor. The strategic plan is what the investors are investing in. They expect the plan to be executed so that it will deliver a certain cash-flow stream. Marketing plays a key role by helping to position the product and by delivering messages to the marketplace in order to generate sales and profits. In an ideal world, the marketing investments would be very specific and deliver exactly as planned—this is what the marketing machine strives toward.

The annual plan

The company must develop an annual plan of specific actions of how the business and marketing will operate. Shareholders fund the annual plan based on their expectation that it will deliver sales and profit achievement as the executives in the company promise. As opposed to an annual plan, a strategic plan is relatively general and doesn't necessarily include any of the specific market factors that may take place during the annual corporate reporting cycle. The annual plan ties into the strategic plan and fleshes it out. Shareholders trust in both the strategic plan (the vision for the company) as well as the ability of the company to execute against the annual plan. It is this combination that provides the value to the shareholder and sustains their willingness to invest in the company.

The rolling plan

In order to improve the chances of achieving the annual plan, a rolling marketing plan, updated either on a weekly or monthly basis, rolls up into the annual plan. In this way, the original shareholder investment is directly linked to the strategic plan and indirectly linked to the annual plan and rolling plan. The shareholder not only invests in the possibility of a bright future, but also in the company's ability to execute on their plans. The rolling plan plays a key role in this process.

Owning the future

In any organization, whose job is it to capture and funnel all available information concerning the next 90 days and the next 365 days? The marketer's. The marketer must own the future. Sales owns the now by taking orders, finance owns the past by tracking what happened, but marketing owns the future. In order for the marketing machine to be successful, the marketer must set the direction and then look for anything that might impact achievement against that objective.

The marketer must follow each key competitor, industry trend, and consumer trend. Following these trends and immediately building any deviations into the marketing machine will allow the marketing team to make certain that the product/brand's future will unfold as expected. Each marketer will be able to reduce uncertainty and risk in the corporate projections and deliver on the profit and revenue projections. The company revenue and profit will grow as expected and the share price will grow accordingly.

Agility vs. complacency

Brand managers, yours and your competitors, are paid to disrupt. If they aren't disrupting they are complacent. They are paid to see an opportunity and take the risk and go for it. They are paid to demand from their team and their agencies to look for opportunities to change the market. Just as disruptive marketing can change an industry, so too, does complacent marketing. It's just in the negative.

Strategic agility

Complacency comes in many forms and market share leaders are often the most complacent. They have the most to lose and yet surprisingly are often the most complacent. Unless a new innovation can significantly increase volumes, being the market leader means that developing a new product that is less expensive, with more features offered at a lower price generates lower revenues and lower profits. Whether that new product is developed internally or by the competition, it generally means loss in revenues and profits for the market leader.

A little-known fact about Kodak was that, in 1975, they were one of the original inventors of the digital camera. Unfortunately, widespread use of digital cameras would lead directly to less use of film and photographic paper. Today, the market for film or print paper is miniscule. With the resolution of digital camera sensors having now surpassed the resolution of analog film technologies, film products are almost non-existent. Surprisingly, though with the advent of having digital cameras everywhere, the number of pictures being snapped has skyrocketed. Having lost the battle of digital imaging, Kodak filed for bankruptcy in 2013 and is now primarily active in digital printing, graphics and commercial films. They are now only a specialty provider of film for the consumer market. On the other hand, throughout the '80s and '90s, agility was exemplified in Microsoft. This was especially apparent with Bill Gates's internal "Internet Tidal Wave" memo of May 26, 1995.[21] In one swift action the company focus was shifted from

---

[21] http://www.lettersofnote.com/2011/07/internet-tidal-wave.html, October 2016.

desktop software and local area networks to the Internet. He instructed the company to "assign the Internet the highest level of importance." In one of the most valuable companies in the world, this act pulled top-level resources off ongoing projects and moved them to internet-centric projects. Had Microsoft followed Kodak's complacency, they would have continued to develop great desktop products but been sideswiped by the exploding growth of the Internet. Based on this one strategically agile decision, the company was able to develop the market-leading internet browser and many other technologies that fueled and continue to fuel online services.

The Microsoft and Kodak examples represent agile decision-making at its best and worst; it goes to the core of the survival of the company. Agility in marketing, however, needs to take place at all levels in the marketing chain. It needs to take place strategically at the corporate level, and it needs to take place at the tactical and execution level.

Avoiding complacency

Gillette had a problem when sales revenue topped out with the new Fusion razor in the early 2000s. Throughout the process of delivering multi-bladed razors, Gillette employed an Eat-Your-Babies strategy. Without resting on their laurels, Gillette decided to eat their babies by successively replacing their current wildly successful products with even more technologically advanced products. When it was introduced in 1971, the Trac II two-blade razor was an incredible advance and provided an extraordinary shave. Then came the Mach 3 in 1998, which ate their baby - the Trac II. Not only was the shave vastly improved, the blades remained sharp for an incredibly long time. Then—astoundingly—in 2005 they were able to cram five great blades into the Mach 5, and later the Fusion razor, and the shave got even better. Was there a Mach 6 or 7 in our future? When was there going to be an end to this ever-increasing blade count with ever increasing shave quality? And then came the Fusion Proglide Power Razor with Flexball™ Technology. This represents the latest feature set leading to an even better shave. There's no doubt that Gillette owns the shave technology race.

Now Gillette needs to win in the channel. Dollar Shave Club, Harry's, and a few others are taking them on in the channel through a unique automatic monthly fulfillment program. Although their blades may not be as technologically sophisticated, they still offer a great shave, but now with shopping convenience. For a very low charge and with enormous convenience, once a month the shaving clubs send a new set of razors. Gillette responded with the Gillette Shave Club. With a very low cost of shipping, replacement blades arrive at your doorstep every 30 days. Gillette has now responded, but will it be too late? Can convenience with a good shave compensate for a great shave at a higher price?

Marketers need to foresee trends in the marketplace and capitalize on them. These trends can come from anywhere, be they in new media channels, new distribution channels, or new pricing schemes.

Annual planning agility

Agility provides many advantages as well. For marketers, improved annual planning may mean improved negotiation options during the annual upfronts. It may mean that marketing budgets can be more reliable engines of growth as opposed to sinks of expense. It may mean better investment in the right marketing technology infrastructure—and much more. The best marketing planning provides the most options at the latest possible moment to achieve the best outcomes at the least cost and least risk.

For the CEO

Taking place in the spring, the "upfronts" are a series of events put on by television networks to sell their Fall programming to advertisers so that the best rates can be achieved and advertising volume commitments can be made. Recently, the upfronts have also led to a parallel series of events to sell high volumes of digital advertising space, taking place about one month after the television upfronts.

Marketers need to build agility specifically into their annual plans. Can they underspend in one reporting period but be allowed to overspend in the next? Accountants, for good reason, would prefer not to see wild, unplanned swings in what they would term expense spending. If their goal is to present results to shareholders with continuously growing revenue and profit growth, having one month of low marketing expense followed by a month of high marketing expense would be anathema to their goal. The marketing reserve as described above is one way to avoid this and build agility into the annual marketing plan. It allows the marketing team the opportunity to overspend without having to be tied down to an overly complex and burdensome spending approval process. It means that the marketing plan must be conceived and approved to meet the corporate sales goal with another 15% or 20% in reserve to accommodate potential bad months or capitalize on good opportunities as they arise.

A common way to build agility is to plan for retail seasonal fluctuations, which are enormous at year-end in the U.S. due to the Christmas shopping season. In China, seasonal fluctuations are dependent on the Chinese New Year. Accountants can easily explain these seasonal fluctuations and stockholders are willing to accept them. Use of the marketing reserve is an unplanned (as to when) but planned for (as to amount) aberration in marketing expenses, a logical extension of this principle. Accounting will need to accrue for this expenditure so that it can be evenly spread across all months. In this way, swings in marketing expenses don't appear as a short-term spike in overall marketing expenses.

Marketing does need to be careful not to simply spend their reserve every month in order to reduce the risk of not making their numbers. The reserve is meant to be a *one-time* budget infusion in response to an unforeseen event in the marketplace that would cause projected revenues to fall short of target.

Agility is also built into the marketing plan through the development and tracking of the right interim variables. These are known as key performance indicators (KPIs) and if designed appropriately, reflect how the marketing team is achieving their objectives at each level in the purchase funnel. With the right KPIs in place, the company can quickly foresee possible trends working against them or in their favor. With the wrong KPIs in place and without an appropriate level of agility, the company may miss a key trend that will cause them to miss the month, the quarter, or even the year. For example, the number of sunny days in a summer month is one KPI that can easily impact overall demand in the sunscreen category. If there are fewer sunny days, the demand for sunscreen may decline. To keep sales on track for the month, marketing may need to respond with more advertising or promotions.

KPIs need to be centered on consumer purchase behavior. They need to track as best as possible where the consumer is in their purchase cycle. Competitive, channel, and external factors that may impact overall demand in the category must also be tracked.

Tactical agility

Consumers have disposable income that can be saved or spent. Marketers can shift consumer disposable income to their advantage in many ways. With the dynamic environment of the Internet, new options for reaching consumers appear just about every day. In 2016, Pokémon Go, an augmented reality game, exploded onto the scene and was able to generate over $500 million in revenue and over 500 million downloads in its first 60 days of existence.[22] Some consumer brands quickly added locations to their marketing so that players would spend more time near or in their stores through PokeStops. (PokeStops are virtual landmarks where players can collect points and characters.[23]) McDonald's and other major brands even worked to incorporate the game into major new marketing campaigns. Whether Pokémon Go can provide long-term marketing opportunities is still to be determined, but for now, having the flexibility to jump on the Pokémon Go bandwagon as soon as possible provided significant marketing opportunities for many consumer brands.

Marketers need the agility to see these opportunities, weigh their potential value, and then quickly respond to them in order to deliver enhanced returns while they are still possible and before they fade into the level of everyday returns.

Many new short- and long-term opportunities come about on the Internet. When Facebook first launched, it provided nearly free access to many eyeballs in a new format. The brands that jumped on first were able to generate great results. Then when Facebook changed its messaging methodology (the EdgeRank Algorithm[24]) to where major brands could no longer reach their fans without paying for post promotion, the ROI of posting without promotion on Facebook declined significantly. With the EdgeRank Algorithm in place, the brands could no longer be guaranteed of reaching all their fans, whether they posted 100 times or 1,000 times. Even with this decline, Facebook still offers excellent returns over and above many other paid media channels. If you were a brand agile enough to jump on the

---

[22] http://www.ibtimes.com/pokemon-go-generates-500-million-revenue-record-time-even-usage-slows-2413914, October 2016.

[23] http://www.adweek.com/news/technology/yogurt-brand-found-clever-workaround-get-front-pokemon-go-players-172671, October 2016.

[24] Facebook's EdgeRank Algorithm determined which fans would receive a post. Generally, it was based on the volume and recency of interaction between fans and brands. The lower the volume and the lower the recency, the less likely a post would be forwarded to the fan. For major brands, in a move to generate advertising revenue, the current Facebook algorithm limits the number of posts transmitted to their fans to less than 1%.

Facebook marketing channel early on, you were able to reap better rewards. If you weren't, your brand sales would not have grown as fast as those brands that did capitalize on this new media channel.

Initially, opportunities like Facebook, or recently Pokémon Go, provided short-term competitive advantage over the less agile competitor. Long term, Facebook continues to provide value to the early agile marketer as those marketers built up both a strong, large fan base and years of experience in the channel. They are now seen as innovative, social-media active brands. They are reaping the rewards of this past agility. Those brands that came late to Facebook need to invest more now in order to achieve the same fan-base size and act on the activation opportunities that a larger fan base provides.[25]

Similarly, marketers late to the Pokémon Go party will have also incurred higher investment costs playing catch-up against the early agile marketers that invested early in the experience and associated reputation.

Tactical agility doesn't have to be just media-channel centric. Agility in pricing and distribution channels is also important. In 1991, being able to develop and implement new pricing options allowed MCI to develop a competitive advantage with its "Friends & Family" pricing. When this pricing was first introduced, it was estimated by the company that it would take over 6 months for the competition to offer a similar pricing scheme.[26] This agility on the side of MCI provided a short-term, highly valuable competitive advantage. Due to their lethargic nature, the competition (AT&T and US Sprint) would need many months to be able to imitate. AT&T initially even disparaged the pricing scheme as "using our customers as salespeople for our products."[27]

Agility in the distribution channel is also disrupting many industries. With the move to 24/7 product access through the Internet, having an online store provides significant new revenue streams. Similarly, as the shift

---

[25] Although there is some debate as to the value of a large fan base, larger fan bases provide some value in the ability for brands to effectively reach their customer base. Having no fans is clearly of little value. It means that there is no option to deliver promoted posts to a brand's fans. It also means that they can't learn from their fans through look-alike analyses and other analytics options.

[26] http://articles.chicagotribune.com/1991-03-19/business/9101250124_1_mci-customers-discount-plan-residential-long-distance-customers, October 2016.

[27] Ibid. Oriano Pagnucci, an AT&T spokesman.

from desktop to mobile internet access unfolds, the brands with the most mobile-friendly sites and best e-commerce functions will see improved sales revenue through the online channel. Marketers need to be agile across all 4Ps of the marketing mix.

Improved annual marketing planning

The best plans provide the best estimate of future events and prepare the best actions to capitalize on those events. The best plans plan for what's known and allow contingencies for what might happen. There are seven key planning components that are critical to building an agile plan:

1. Accommodating seasonality
2. Preparing for trends
3. Preparing for stochastic variability (e.g., weather)
4. Preparing for known channel and external factor(s)
5. Preparing for unknown channel and external factor(s)
6. Preparing for possible competitive thrust(s)
7. Preparing for own thrust(s)

Accommodating seasonality

There are many causes of seasonal variation in demand. Some can be internal, some external.

Internal variability refers to the variability built in by the sales team given strong monthly and quarterly achievement incentives. As the sales team acts to achieve the numbers for the month or the quarter, activity rises at the end of the month and end of the quarter, but then also slows at the beginning of the month and beginning of the quarter. This produces a heartbeat of demand and revenue.

Quarterly Sales Heartbeat

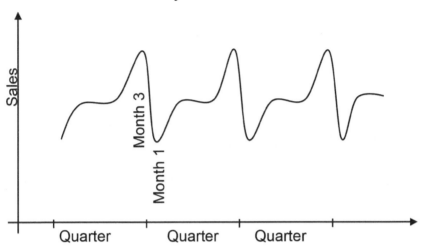

Figure 5: Heartbeat of month end sales

Annual plant shutdowns can also create internal variability. Shutdowns in the auto industry take place for the model year changeover and/or during year-end holidays. These shutdowns can cause related industry seasonalities or, for the auto dealers, spikes and troughs in inventory.

External sources of seasonality include holidays and special occasions such as back-to-school, Christmas holidays, and the Chinese New Year. Seasonality also occurs due to annual trade shows for B2B marketers. Many industry-wide trade shows take place once per year and demand and lead generation are at their strongest during this time. For example, the Consumer Electronics Show is at the beginning of the year, while the Hannover Messe in Germany is in the Spring. Annual events such as these typically lead to a spike in demand and sales activity. Marketers need to plan their other activities around these spikes in order to deliver a more continuous flow of leads and sales based on the sum of all marketing activities throughout the year.

External variability can also come from other sources, such as the growing season for agricultural products. The harvest can only take place at certain times of the year yielding highly seasonal sales during the harvest period.

Seasonality doesn't have to occur on an annual basis. It can occur over multiple years. There is always a relationship between the Olympics and global alcohol sales, the presidential election cycle and advertising prices in the U.S.

Preparing for trends

Preparing for trends has some nuances to it as well. Will the shift from traditional trade to modern trade in emerging economies grow at 9%, 10%, or 11%? When will it begin to level off—or will it accelerate? Depending on the industry, marketers will need to run different scenarios to determine the incremental impact from each of these scenarios and then act accordingly. But they will also need to build in contingencies (against which they should be ready to apply their marketing reserve) in order to make certain the trends don't negatively impact their ability to both make the numbers and provide consistent and continuous revenue and profits as per expectations of the stockholders.

Preparing for stochastic variability (e.g., weather)

There are many variables that are outside of the control of the marketer, yet generate unforeseen variability in demand. For businesses that are weather-dependent, such as carbonated beverages, an extraordinarily warm or cold summer will impact sales either in a positive or negative way. The marketer, however, has a few options to make certain the plans are achieved, regardless of the weather.

Planning for the extreme is one way to guarantee that the revenue targets are achieved, but this may lead to overspending and reduced profits in the case of a cold summer. Building a plan for average weather based on some projection of past variability and trends, yet also building in a contingency for worst case scenarios, may provide a better alternative. This alternative may provide the best chance to make the revenue numbers, with a lower risk of missing the profit numbers. Or the company can choose to make the profit numbers and miss the revenue numbers.

Preparing for known external factors

In many cases, changes in the industry are known well in advance. Technology changes such as the launch of a new PC microprocessor from Intel may be known months or years in advance. New regulatory changes are usually phased in with a known schedule. These types of changes often represent step changes in market dynamics. Variability in their expected impact and in their timing are crucial contingencies that marketers must account for. Marketers that can best prepare for these step changes will be the most successful in the market. With these step changes come uncertainties as to the market response. In order to make certain the brand will achieve their numbers, agile marketers need to develop scenarios for each happenstance in order to be prepared to achieve the best overall results.

Preparing for unknown external factors

Unknown factors can be major or minor. If there are a lot of factors that impinge on a specific industry, these can be treated like stochastic variability, as described above.

Major unknown factors, such as a product recall or product failure, may not be able to be accounted for by marketing. Here are three examples that had a significant impact on the business and their share prices:

Boeing Dreamliner battery problems[28,29]

The Boeing 787 Dreamliner was a marvel in aviation technology. It utilized new materials and offered significant fuel savings and passenger amenities and comfort. Unfortunately, Boeing ran into problems with their lithium batteries. The battery flaws led to electrical fires, leading to a grounding of the plane until the battery overheating problems could be rectified. This slowed orders and delivery of orders, leading to a significant share price decline. Share prices rebounded a year later once the battery problems appeared to be solved and order backlogs grew.

---

[28] http://www.chicagobusiness.com/article/20150520/BLOGS10/ 150519773/boeings-787-bet-finally-pays-off, October 2016.
[29] http://www.nytimes.com/2014/12/02/business/report-on-boeing-787-dreamliner-batteries-assigns-some-blame-for-flaws.html, October 2016.

Samsung Galaxy Note 7 smartphone battery problems

In August 2016, Samsung released its new Galaxy Note 7 smartphone ahead of the competitive Apple iPhone 7 launch in September of the same year. This normally would have been seen as a coup—delivering advanced features ahead of the launch of the market-leading iPhone series. There was one problem: The batteries started overheating, causing small explosions and sometimes catching fire. The FAA ruled that these phones weren't allowed to be turned on during flights and finally Samsung issued a recall of all of the phones.

In a case like this, marketers may only be able to respond by promoting the brand's other phones to make up for the interruption in revenues from this otherwise successful product. The interruption in revenue took place just as the Apple iPhone 7 was launched to great Apple-style fanfare. If the consumer is now temporarily without a phone for a handful of weeks, they would need to use an alternative. They could swap it for a replacement, or get a refund from Samsung and purchase the Apple iPhone 7 or some other product. If it was some other competitive product, these sales would be lost forever to Samsung. The product has now been fully removed from the market and the total cost of the product failure is in the many billions of dollars.

Volkswagen diesel engine emission scandal

In September 2015, the U.S. Environmental Protection Agency issued a notice of a violation of the Clean Air Act by the German company Volkswagen through software manipulation of engine emissions during testing that gave an inaccurate depiction of emissions during normal driving. About 11 million cars worldwide were affected. The car exhibited extraordinary fuel efficiency and power, over and above other competitive diesel models, but at the cost of air quality. It is estimated that a few hundred deaths may have been caused by the increased pollution from these cars.

It took several months for the impact of the fraudulent software to be determined, but it was massive. Total costs to Volkswagen are estimated to be in the tens of billions of dollars.[30] The loss in shareholder value was reflected by a $30 loss in share price once the scandal became widely known.[31]

These three examples are the extreme, and most likely can't be adequately compensated for by any marketing. Agile marketing may be able to mitigate some of the losses when there is a major external event, but, in most cases, never makes up for the total losses to the business. However, agile marketing *will* allow the company to quickly explore its options so it can develop new plans as to how best to respond. In Volkswagen's case, immediately following the scandal, they began promoting a green agenda and began heavy advertising to mitigate losses to the brand and promote their non-diesel engine models. Since then they have been able to capture the top spot in global car production long held by Toyota and, prior to that, GM.

Preparing for possible competitive thrusts

Your competitors have several weapons up their sleeves to disrupt the market, and their brand managers are incentivized to do just that. They can introduce new products, introduce new pricing schemes, change the rules in the distribution channel, or develop new creative that takes the market by storm. Agile marketers can prepare in advance for these potential outcomes so that they can more quickly respond to the competitive thrust and mitigate the potential losses due to these disruptions. Here are two examples of market disrupting actions:

Branding: Dove campaign for real beauty

The Dove Campaign for Real Beauty was launched in 2004 after a 3-year market research study uncovered that only 2% of women felt that they were beautiful. This lack of self-esteem led to a multi-year campaign that took the world by storm and left competitors in their wake. Because most of the personal care categories in which Dove competed were filled with many near-equal competitors, the campaign itself had a proportionately near-equal impact on all competitors in the respective categories. The campaign didn't

---

[30] http://www.autoexpress.co.uk/volkswagen/92893/vw-emissions-scandal-recalls-compensation-is-your-car-affected-latest-news, October 2016.
[31] https://uk.finance.yahoo.com/echarts?s=VOW.DE#symbol=VOW.DE; range=2y, October 2016.

go directly after one competitor in particular, so to recover lost sales, competitors only had to make up for the recovery of their proportionate loss in sales.

Distribution channel: Dell selling PCs over the Internet

Michael Dell launched his computer company by providing a great product with a streamlined supply chain extending all the way through to its sales function. Initially, Dell PCs could only be purchased through its website, whereas other PCs were sold through expensive face-to-face salesforces or through retail stores. This streamlined approach led Dell Computer to become one of the market leaders through the 1990s and into the early 2010s.

At the time, IBM sold mostly through their expensive face-to-face salesforce, making it difficult for them to compete on price and delivery. Had they been agile, they would have seen the impact of this new channel and been able to respond in a much timelier fashion.

Media seasonality and predictability

Competitive marketing campaigns often follow a certain seasonality. Although the market may not be tied to a certain seasonal demand cycle, they nevertheless advertise with a seasonal cycle. They are strong during certain months and weak during others. These types of competitors are very easy to plan against. There may be a question as to what media mix or creative campaign they use, but the regularity and predictability of their media expenditures make it very easy to develop effective competitive plans. When the competitor has a more random approach it is much more difficult to plan against; this can lead to wild swings in revenue that would otherwise need to be mitigated.

Whether it's a seasonal price promotion, a seasonal media campaign, or some other action, each competitive action has an impact on sales. Being prepared means that the marketer develops counter-strategies that can be tested ahead of time and are ready to be put in place should the need arise. Marketers need to build response packages that have been optimized for each potential competitive action. They need to have tested and optimized them so that a quick turn-around is possible. In this way agility is built into the marketing plan. For example, it may have been possible for the impact from the highly successful Dove Campaign for Real Beauty to have been mitigated through a new pricing strategy. The Dell online sales channel may have been mitigated in the short term through price rebates combined with a strong media campaign while the company took time to build out its own online sales and fulfillment channel. To counteract a competitor's unpredictable media execution, determining potential response requirements in advance goes a long way to being able to quickly respond in a timely manner once their campaign begins.

Responding in a timely way

In many industries, a response can't be executed in a single day. Placing television media in the short term can be done at a high price using spot TV, but it can be bought at a lower price when there is more time to react. Digital on the other hand can be purchased almost overnight, providing the marketer a new very short-term channel to deliver messages when needed.

Price changes can't be executed overnight either. For many retailers, price changes can mean a lot of rework at the shelves. They are sometimes costly to implement and may lead to lost revenue and bad relations with the retailer's other suppliers. Also, making a blanket price change may lead to a price war, so responses based on price need to be carefully considered; the timing and other aspects need to be carefully scrutinized if they are to be part of the response package.

Changes in distribution are even more difficult to implement in the short term. Getting more shelf space may simply be impossible, or it may be too costly due to the required flooring charges retailers may impose. Short-term in-store promotions through an increase in features or displays may also be impossible since every other manufacturer in the grocery channel wants this same opportunity.

Because of these structural constraints, having the response package in place can allow for an overall quicker execution of the required response once the need for execution becomes apparent. Predefined response packages for common potential changes in the marketplace, whether they're media-, pricing- or distribution-related, allow the marketer to implement changes with a short turnaround when they become necessary.

In summary, if marketing wants to develop a marketing machine where revenue can be expected in a regular and consistent way, they need to make certain their plans accommodate potential levels of uncertainty.

Preparing for own thrust(s)

Planning with agility for a major marketing initiative of your own, such as a product launch, is important; there are often interdependencies between existing product revenue and the initiative. One of the biggest challenges is determining the impact on volume of existing products once the new product is brought to the market. Not only are there interdependencies, but sales of existing products are also expected to be maintained in parallel with the sales of the new product. For most businesses, this is almost impossible. The new product launch has often borrowed internal resources and manpower from the existing product, making it more difficult for the existing product's marketing team to respond. The new product is often funded out of the marketing budget of the existing product, so it is almost inevitable that the existing product will decline due to the reduced marketing support. And lastly, many times the existing product with lesser features needs to be reduced in price to maintain the relative value proposition of the new product/price combination.

Even with the best plans, execution never goes exactly as planned—especially for a product launch. Distribution access may be delayed, product availability or shipments may be delayed, or media execution and PR may be shifted out. Each of these unforeseen launch challenges can lead to misalignment and lower-than-expected sales volumes. Then the competition will respond, either in an expected or unexpected way. External factors may also be different than foreseen. Both of these typically lead to reduced and/or delayed sales volumes. In each case, marketers need to be agile and have planned contingencies that can be executed without the friction of protracted approval cycles and delayed spending authority.

How to build a marketing measurement plan

With a marketing machine in place, the marketing campaign planning process should be methodical and self-regulated.

Setting the objectives

Foremost in building a marketing campaign plan is to set out the objectives of the plan. What is the action desired? Should the message recipient call a phone number, visit a website, or just build and reinforce a particular brand image? In addition, secondary actions that might be taken should also be contemplated. If the goal is to build and reinforce the brand image, it should also be expected that during the campaign, message recipients will also visit the brand website and social properties.

Determining the metrics

How will the success of the campaign be measured? How will the marketing team know if the objectives have been met? With a properly implemented marketing machine, the tracking metrics already exist—the question is how this marketing activity will deliver on these metrics, and whether the campaign will achieve the objectives as required by the corporate annual plan.

If the metrics don't exist, the marketing machine may be incomplete. If the metrics don't exist, marketers must find creative ways to capture the appropriate metrics in order to build a robust marketing machine to support their decision making.

Before a campaign begins any important interim and financial success metric for the company should already be defined. Marketers shouldn't necessarily be identifying *new* KPIs with each and every new marketing campaign or media channel. They should already be defined; it is only the various targets for each of these KPIs that need to be defined. Especially for a new experimental marketing activity, the company will need to determine how success will be measured and how that success fits into the overall metrics infrastructure of the marketing machine.

Identify target segments

It is very rare that a campaign targets the entire market. Typically marketing activities target a specific segment. Detailed targeting at the segment level allows the messaging, the timing and the media placements to be properly optimized. It is this targeting that needs to be carefully defined, with measurement methodologies at the segment level put in place to capture the appropriate response data.

Developing the message and the creative

When the target segment has been identified, the message and the creative form in which it will be delivered need to be defined. For example, using psychographic segmentation, putting the message in the right context can have a significant impact on success. For introverted segments, images without many people are more effective. For individuals that are more gregarious, images with a lot of people socializing together work best. A hotel chain implemented the Magic Sauce application from the University of Cambridge and was able to significantly increase conversions through improved targeting and messaging. The application even won Bronze at the Travel Marketing Awards 2016 in the category of "Most Innovative Marketing Campaign."[32]

Testing the message and the creative

A critical step in the successful implementation of a marketing machine is the testing regimen of marketing messages and creative concepts. Regardless of how good the creative team is, the actual response in the market by real consumers should be the final arbiter of the actual implemented messaging. After messages and creative concepts are developed, these can be easily tested either through market research or by online A/B testing to determine which variants perform the best.

Determining the timing and frequency

Marketing campaigns are always very timing-dependent, either because of seasonalities or because of internal timing requirements, such as the launch of a new product. Once complete, a marketing model can help to optimize all of the components of the marketing activity by simulating and optimizing how they interact to best achieve the desired outcome. Optimization includes the timing between each element of the marketing mix and the weight of each element. For example, a new product launch may be more successful if the product is first made available on the shelves, followed by an awareness campaign accompanied by a trial generating campaign through digital and in-store coupons. The best models can improve the marketing mix and media sequencing of most launches by 10–20%.

---

[32] https://www.psychometrics.cam.ac.uk/client-showcase/grayling, August 27, 2017.

> **Big Algorithms in the realm of Big Data**
>
> Not only has the growth of new data sources exploded, but so, too, has the plethora of new algorithms exploded to handle these new exponentially growing volumes of data. Traditional methods to analyze enormous data sets can work but may take weeks or months to process. Marketers need answers in a few seconds or a few milliseconds. This processing time crunch means that marketing analysts must find and apply new algorithms that can deliver great answers in a fraction of the time.

Making marketing agility agile.

Agile marketers must not only be agile in their marketing, but in the whole process of agility itself. Agility also needs continuous improvement. This can take place along four dimensions:

1. **Searching for new data sets** – New data sources deliver value in several ways. They help marketers better target their consumers or they can provide better response measurement to track marketing success.

2. **Searching for new algorithms** – Trends in technology allow faster computing times and higher computing power. Each of these is easily scalable through many of the cloud-computing platforms (e.g., Microsoft Azure, Amazon Web Services, and Google Cloud Service), but data volumes seem to march forward even faster. These trends are expected to continue. In parallel with the data and infrastructure trends, innovative new algorithms are required to be able to process these ever-growing volumes of data in new ways and in shorter and shorter timeframes.

3. **Continuous improvement to the process, automating where possible** – Workflows are never perfect. They must be continuously improved. Staffing changes and disruptions in the market require that the workflows evolve and adjust. Some workflows can be automated in such a way to save time and remove rote work, freeing up time for analytic and strategic creativity.

4. **Seeking better support of the creative process** – Great processes can significantly improve any marketing organization, but great

creative is at the core of marketing greatness. The Aflac duck, the Coca Cola polar bears, Apple's 1984 Macintosh commercial, and many other creative concepts will be remembered for decades and longer. The marketing machine and the way marketing supports the creative process must be agile and work to develop new ways to provide even greater insight into the decision-making processes of the consumer. From there, marketers can capitalize on that agility to own the future and begin to share the marketing machine with the rest of the company.

Section Three:
Marketing Owns the Future

Chapter 7

There Are Many Futures
There Are Many Owners

Owning the future means being responsible for planning the corporate actions to achieve the required sales for that period. It means identifying the actions that must take place today—and in the future—to make certain that the company is in the best position possible to be able to achieve sales expectations at a later date. The further into the future we look, the more uncertain that future is. There are many forces working in our favor, many working against us. It is up to the future's owner to have a clear vision of what might happen and what *can* happen in order to be prepared with the right actions and the right spending authority to achieve the corporate plan.

Who owns what part of the future?

Some of the ownership of the future is shared with the CEO, some with the sales team. Of course, other groups within the company deliver on what's sold and provide services, but from a marketing perspective, the future is a shared responsibility between the sales team, marketing, and the CEO. As we look at the very near future, marketing has joint ownership with sales. Depending on the company, marketing may even relinquish full ownership of what takes place in the very short term. Throughout any period further out into the future, the sales team has less and less ownership, whereas the marketing team has more and more ownership.

Though there is always input from sales and marketing peering out into the long-term, the long-term future is owned by the CEO. For a multi-brand company, it is owned by the most senior brand manager. (In that case the

CEO is meant here as the CEO of the brand.) The farthest possible view into the future is the vision for the company. The corporate or brand vision is owned by the CEO; in the end he or she is also the owner of the risk associated with that vision. The further into the future we peer, the more our planning is defined by this vision. The CEO needs to weigh what is known about what the organization can deliver—given estimates of what can generally be possible and given estimates of what the competition may be able to deliver—and what impediments any external factors or the channel may place in the company's way. All of this is tempered by the level of investment the company's vision can deliver. It may be that the vision is theoretically perfect, but if it isn't a vision that can garner an investor then it isn't viable. The vision must be able to justify investment given the estimated risk levels for the estimated returns based on the value of the vision. Just as the rest of the company must justify their portion of the budget, so too, does the corporate vision need to justify its portion of the investment in the stock market.

Subdividing the future

There are five dimensions of the future that must be owned. It can be subdivided down into the next few seconds all the way up into the next 3 to 5 years or longer.

The next few minutes to the next 24 hours

For some businesses, the next few seconds and minutes are critical. In search engine marketing, second-by-second decisions are made to determine the level of investment needed to bid on the best keywords. Online gambling is one industry that optimizes keyword tactics on a real-time basis.

The next week

Its dynamics demand that many businesses' online marketing operates on a weekly basis. Marketing has full ownership of the coming week, delivering short-term messages and moving visitors to the website and/or to the company's sales channels, whether they're online or in brick and mortar.

For the CEO

Search-engine marketing is one of the most dynamic opportunities any company has: to capitalize on an individual's purchase behavior as expressed through their online search behavior. As individuals search online for answers or for specific offers, they place key words or phrases into the search engines (e.g., Google and Bing). On the other side of the equation, marketers position their company by purchasing key words in the search-engines to generate the most exposure and clicks for the least amount of money. The higher they bid for these keywords, the higher these companies appear in the rankings.

If consumers are searching for travel ideas, being found in the sponsored section of the search results (at the top and to the right of the results page) is important, though it is ideal to be in the organic first-page results as well. Appearing on the second page often means not being found. To a large extent, especially for high-value search terms, appearing on that first page determines whether the company website will be seen. For example, the most expensive keyword/phrase bid in March 2016 in Google as per SEMRush was *best mesothelioma lawyer* at $935.71 per click.[1] The next nine were:

$425.70	Dallas truck accident lawyer
$411.04	truck accident lawyer Houston
$393.79	Louisville car accident lawyer
$388.84	Houston 18-wheeler accident lawyer
$381.65	San Diego water damage
$377.70	are personal injury settlements taxable
$361.34	Baltimore auto accident lawyer
$358.11	accident lawyer Sacramento
$358.03	car accident lawyer Phoenix

[1] https://www.clickz.com/the-100-most-expensive-google-adwords-keywords-in-the-us/100937/, September 2016.

The next 30 to 90 days

In order to reliably deliver on the corporate plan, the monthly and, especially, the quarterly numbers are at the heart of the commitment the company has to its shareholders. If the company fails to meet or exceed the corporate monthly and quarterly numbers just a few times, the team will fail and heads will roll. Although they differ from company to company, a weekly rolling 30-day plan or 90-day plan, or a monthly rolling 90-day plan, are typically designed to incorporate the next 30- or 90-day future. Sales owns the next 30- and 90-day planning periods.

The annual plan

Often the annual plan is given a strategic moniker (marketing says everything they do is strategic), even though it is really just the senior management team negotiating on what they can deliver given their estimate of the future, the competitive environment and channel and external factors, and their ability to execute. Based on their estimates and the demands of the investors (the shareholders), they commit to the annual plan. Typically, the plan turns into budgetary authority for each of the departments to act against, assuming the top-line numbers are achieved. If those numbers aren't achieved, spending throughout the company is often delayed or cut back. As long as the sales commitments are met, the likelihood is high that the budgeted spending authority will be allowed to progress.

Companies will often augment the annual plan with a rolling 12-month plan, which is slightly different from the annual plan. The annual plan is what the company commits to the board and to the shareholders. The rolling plan gets updated every month, so that as conditions in the market change, the company can adjust its plan to still meet and exceed the corporate annual plan. A 12-month rolling plan is one of the best ways to keep the marketing and selling functions fully aligned, especially in businesses where the sales cycles stretch to greater than a few months. Sales, marketing, and the CEO jointly own the annual plan.

The next 3 to 5 years or longer

This timeframe can truly be defined as strategic. This 3-to-5-year vision is owned by the CEO. Nevertheless, marketing also has a clear voice into the ongoing development and refinement of the company vision. It is up to the CEO to build this vision of where the company is going based on his/her assessment of the competitive and environmental threats and opportunities. It is the vision and the company's ability to execute on the vision that is sold to the investors as they choose one investment over another. Just as marketers compete with other products in the marketplace and executives compete for budget, so too, does this vision compete against other visions.

It is the quality of this vision that is part of the investor decision matrix, determining the level of investment the company can and will receive from those investors.

Ownership of the future means taking responsibility and accountability for the company's ability to achieve the numbers in that timeframe. In most organizations, especially in B2B, the sales team has the ultimate responsibility: to achieve the numbers in the now every month. But in reality, best-in-class companies' marketing plays an equal if not *superordinate* role in achieving the numbers the further out into the future the company looks. It is marketing's role to set the company up for success so that the sales team has the best chance of achieving the numbers at least cost and least risk. As we've seen in this section, the rolling planning process is the best way to do that.

Chapter 8

The Rolling Planning Process

Improving outcomes is always critical—certainly a necessity for any business. Immutable and inflexible plans, however, can be the bane of a company's existence. The future is always uncertain and being stuck with an immutable plan is the reason for many company's underperformance. Given that we only have limited and imperfect insight into the future, we now know that we need to have a planning method that allows us to make rapid adjustments to those plans without the molasses of cumbersome approvals slogging through the veins of the organization. Not only would a slow decision cycle reduce the ability to respond, but it can also reduce the creativity of the final activation in the market. Imagine if Oreo had to have high-level approval for its "You can still dunk in the dark" tweet.[33]

Oreo's dunk in the dark

During the 2014 Super Bowl game between the San Francisco 49ers and the Baltimore Ravens, the stadium experienced an unexpected blackout lasting about 30 minutes. In the middle of the short blackout, as the teams stood around on the field waiting for the power to come back on, the Oreo brand's fast-thinking social marketing agency, 360i, tweeted the now famous tweet: "You can still dunk in the dark" (https://twitter.com/Oreo/status/298246571718483968/photo/1?ref_src=twsrc%5Etfw). This one tweet led to 10,000 retweets in the first hour and many more as the day wore on. The tweet was written up as a brilliant stroke for the Oreo brand, leading to many, many more impressions and positive feedback and accolades for the brand.

---

[33] Source: http://www.huffingtonpost.com/2013/02/04/oreos-super-bowl-tweet-dunk-dark_n_2615333.html

Figure 6: Oreo has an Award-Winning Tweet, "You can still dunk in the dark"

Marketers need a fast turn-around cycle on decisions regarding both content and budget. Depending on the dynamism in the category, rolling planning, either with a weekly or monthly cycle, can provide the agility necessary to be ahead of the category in order to make the best decisions possible.

As discussed in previous chapters, marketers have begun building marketing models to optimize their marketing mixes. These models can be simple, providing optimization of the top media channels, or they can be complete consumer-centric models providing deep insights into how consumers make purchase decisions. In either case, these models are at the core of the marketing machine. With these models, marketers can optimize their media investments and generate higher revenue and ROI from their marketing budgets. But these models can be much more valuable. They can significantly enhance the rolling planning process by providing the basis for the optimization of the marketing mix for each rolling plan.

Because the fiscal quarterly numbers are so important for most organizations, the planning horizon should stretch to be equal to or just longer than a quarter. This allows the rolling planning process to incorporate what must be done on a weekly or monthly basis to meet or exceed the fiscal quarterly numbers. This means the rolling planning cycle should look out either 3 or 4 months for a monthly rolling planning cycle, or 13 or 16 weeks for a weekly rolling planning cycle. This look ahead should also be long enough to encompass any specific media planning decisions that may have a longer lead time than the 90 days in a quarter.

The rolling planning process encompasses 5 primary steps:

1. Measuring results in the marketplace
2. Capturing and re-forecasting both own/competitive and channel/external factor data
3. Updating the marketing model and re-verifying that the model is (still) predictive with the latest data (from step 1 and 2)
4. Re-forecasting and optimizing own and competitive projections based on latest actual and forecasted competitive and environmental data
5. Executing the updated plan

1. Measuring results in the marketplace

Success measurements come from many sources. Measurements can be financial, usually in terms of volumes shipped and revenue achieved. These are important if the company is selling directly to the consumer, but less important if the company sells through a distribution channel. In this case, the actual sell-thru representing what the *consumer* purchased is what is important. There are many third-party sources of this data, including Nielsen and IRI for FMCG and R. L. Polk for automotive. This same data can be captured (however, at a much higher cost) through internal primary research.

Interim success metrics providing data throughout the purchase process can also come from many sources. Social media, such as Facebook and Twitter, provide valuable engagement metrics. Web visit behavior can be provided from web analytics tools, such as Adobe Marketing Cloud, IBM Customer Analytics, and Google Analytics. Other data vendors also provide valuable, up-to-the-minute metrics of a company's web presence. Millward Brown, GfK, and other primary market researchers provide valuable brand tracking data indicating brand imagery, awareness, and purchase intent.

All of these inputs and more can be used in a detailed model to help make accurate projections of the future. Unfortunately, not all of these data sets are available at the same time. Some are available nearly instantaneously, others are available only after a lag. For example, brand tracking data may only be available 15 days after the end of the month.

This means that the updated future projection must be able to work with a mix of the most recent measured data and the most recent projections of the future data. If the model is to be updated on the 10th of the month, then it can include actual data from the company's online presence, but only projected data from the company's brand tracker, which will only be available 5 days later. If the un-updated data is a strong signal in the model, then the model projections need to be tested (through sensitivity analysis) over a range of potential values in order to determine the level of output sensitivity and the risk involved with the final recommended rolling marketing plan.

2. Capturing and re-forecasting both own/competitive and channel/external factor data

The biggest unknowns in the marketplace are the plans of the competition. We may be able to track competitive actions in the past, but it is the estimation of their potential actions in the future that can significantly reduce the risk inherent in any agile marketing planning process. As the process gets more embedded in the organization and is practiced over many months, projections of competitive actions can become much more robust. Initially, when the process is first introduced into the organization, the team will be surprised at the wealth of competitive information available but may have trepidation in staking their actions on these estimates. After a few months, the team will get much better at estimating competitive actions and will have confidence in their ability to develop a successful rolling action plan even in the face of uncertainty in their competitive activity assessments.

Depending on the industry, external factors, such as regulatory changes or technology changes, are easier to project. Some are more important than others. Getting the step-function changes, such as start dates of new regulations, both in time and impact, can have a strong influence on the accuracy of future projections. Getting the weather right over the course of the rolling planning cycle is typically less critical, since, on average, the weather (rain, snow, high and low temperatures) will be very similar year after year. Big, stochastic weather events, such as tornadoes or hurricanes, on the other hand, can have localized devastating impact on the accuracy of the projection but are almost impossible to predict and should generally be left out of the equation. Marketers, however, must simply have response packages in place that can be quickly implemented should a major event with significant impact on sales take place.

In order for the projections to be as accurate as possible, these projections must be updated in the rolling planning cadence as new data comes in and the team learns more about what is going on in the marketplace.

Capturing own data is usually straightforward. It is mostly available from the agency (for media data) or internal sources (for pricing and distribution data).

3. Updating the marketing model and re-verifying that the model is (still) predictive with the latest data (from step 1 and 2)

As the latest financial and interim success data becomes available, the model should always be re-verified. Depending on the core methodology in building the model, this process may be simple or complex. Agent-based models provide the best accuracy looking into the future, whereas statistical and other models may require extensive re-working as new success data becomes available. Once the model has been re-verified, the model is ready to run the latest projections and scenarios.

4. Re-forecasting and optimizing own and competitive projections based on latest competitive and environmental data

Once we have the latest actual data and the best competitive projections in place, we can run the model to simulate and optimize against potential scenarios facing us from the competition or from environmental factors. From the simulation results we can now choose the best options given the expected futures and the potential risks associated with each of the modeled scenarios. We can now act in the marketplace.

5. Executing the updated plan

With the model in place, we can now make trade-offs in many dimensions. Not only can we trade-off investments between media channels in the marketing mix, we can also trade-off in time, choosing, for example, digital media now over spot TV, but purchasing cable TV with a longer lead time in order to get the best pricing for the required impact throughout the planning cycle.

This rolling planning process should move from steps 1 to 5 quickly—preferably within a day or two—depending on the complexity of the model, the complexity of the data, and the dynamism in the market. The faster this process can be executed, the more agility the marketing team can demonstrate. If the marketing team is on a weekly rolling planning cadence, the process needs to be completed within a day in order to deliver the best impact in the market.

Within the department, the process is best owned by the marketing operations team, since they are the ones typically best suited for regular execution and tracking.

The agile management decision cycle

In highly dynamic markets and certainly with any of the online media channels, marketers need the ability to make spending authority decisions today—not three weeks from now. They can't be hampered by bureaucracy. The agile management decision cycle has to do with how to get quick access to executive authority to make a spending or market decision. That is, not only could the spending level change, but there could also be a shift in media mix, creative concept, or in-store promotion. To get this right, adjustment authority needs to be provided to allow quick plan modifications without unnecessary bureaucratic largesse or decision delay in the way.

Research & development in marketing: The marketing labs

Opportunities in new media channels become available and disappear very quickly. Sometimes being the first in a new social channel can provide value beyond the simple value of the media impression. As the channel grows in popularity, the ability to attract new eyeballs becomes less and less expensive. If the media channel is unique (for example, as in the augmented reality Pokémon Go mobile game), being associated with the channel early in its existence can deliver higher returns than being a latecomer. Being an early adopter is in the same vein as taking on a sports or music sponsorship. If the sponsored asset is perceived to have similar values and is popular among the brand's target audience, it can be a good payoff. Similarly, for new media channels, the early adopter advertisers have a near sponsorship position in the minds of the target consumer; with this standing, the value of the media channel is much higher than other channels and that value can last a long time, even as the channel grows into a more mainstream brand.

This means that marketers must have the latitude to take chances on new channels and new promotional opportunities as they arise. It means they must have money set aside in their budget to be able to investigate these new channels, test them, and be ready to go into production with them. Marketers need a budget line item to be able to run marketing experiments without a direct link to an outcome. Although there isn't a direct link, the analysis of the media channel needs to be thorough enough that it can be reasonably expected to deliver positive results once an action plan has been developed.

The experimental budget and marketing reserve are both critical for agility. In the next chapter, we will explore the rest of the marketing machine budget and how these pieces fit together.

Chapter 9

Building a Marketing Machine Budget

Marketing machines help companies navigate the budgeting process more smoothly. The traditional give and take is reduced because the level of sales can be dialed in with a reasonable amount of certainty. Nevertheless, there are a few issues to address when building the marketing machine budget.

Marketing budgeting (not including sales)

Marketing budgets are broken down into two primary components: the working media budget and the non-working budget.

Working media (or marketing)

Working media purchases any messages (advertising in all its forms) that are seen or viewed by the consumer. These include television GRPs (Gross Rating Points),[34] radio advertising, digital display advertising, search engine marketing, social media messages, product placements, scents, and many more. The term "message" is used here because it is the unit of measurement that is designed to be seen, heard, or smelled by the consumer. As opposed to mass media, digital and other direct media is generally purchased to reach a specific consumer. Earned media in social platforms such as Facebook and Twitter, on the other hand, is written by consumers and influencers and not directly paid for (although can be promoted through many activities). It delivers positive (and sometimes negative) messages to our consumers. Scent messages are sensed by our consumers as they, for example, walk past our

---

[34] With certain mass media channels, media is purchased based on the number of gross rating points, or percentage of viewing audience. For a detailed description please see: Guy R. Powell, *Marketing Calculator* (Wiley, 2012).

restaurant and the smell of fresh-baked bread is in the air. All of these messages add up to a certain number of impressions received by our consumers, partners, and other stakeholders in the marketplace.

For example, if we wanted to double the level of television advertising, we wouldn't necessarily need to hire more creative designers. We wouldn't need to invest in non-working media (see below), but instead we could simply purchase more GRPs. With that doubling of the television advertising working media, we would have inserted twice the number of messages for the consumers to be exposed to.

Non-working marketing

Non-working marketing is made up of corporate overheads in the marketing department, such as personnel costs, office space, creative design and development, market research, and others. Non-working media are the fixed costs, whereas working media are more variable. Non-working media wouldn't include the costs for social media reps actively monitoring, managing, and promoting the company's social media properties.

For example, if we wanted to invest in market research to improve the creative design, that wouldn't purchase any more messages that would be exposed to consumers. The investment would, however, make the media messages themselves more effective. For this reason, it falls under the marketing budget, but is labeled as "non-working."

Working media and the marketing machine

In order to make the marketing machine viable, we need to separate the marketing investments by how they contribute incremental revenue. With working media investments, there are essentially two types: those that produce hard, certain returns and those that produce softer, less certain returns. Working media are those investments that can be scaled to deliver more messages to the marketplace. For example, if a campaign has 10m impressions on the radio, this investment could be scaled up to 12m or scaled down to 8m impressions without any change to the non-working media budget. Working media costs can include personnel if they are directly tied to scale.

For example, social media representatives or inside sales persons could be scaled up or down.

Hard, certain returns

There are many investments that produce hard, certain returns for the marketer, but they differ by industry. For major national brands, television can produce very certain returns. Television advertising can generate brick-and-mortar as well as online-store visits that convert to sales. Certain channels (such as the Home Shopping Network or QVC) are very effective at providing a very hard and certain link to sales revenue. Television ads can also come in different flavors. Branded television is designed to build the brand, to associate an emotional connection with the brand. The 2015 Budweiser Super Bowl lost dog (Clydesdale/Puppy)[35] commercial is one of these brand building types of ads. Other types of ads are more promotional in nature, such as the Outback Steakhouse commercial for wood-fired grilled favorites.[36]

Branded: Budweiser Clydesdales

---

[35] https://www.youtube.com/watch?v=VWeKtqWc2EA, September 2016
[36] https://www.youtube.com/watch?v=EcITjyMEZjY, September 2016

Branded commercials provide long-term value and are meant to be used in conjunction with other activations. As opposed to ads with a specific call to action, brand-focused commercials generate awareness and build brand equity. These ads provide hard returns, but they provide better returns when activated through other in-store or direct activations leveraging the impact of the brand theme portrayed in the commercial.

Promotional: Outback Steakhouse

Promotional commercials are meant to provide short-term sales. With simple analytics, the sales can easily be tracked to the ad. With a promotion or marketing response code, the direct sales can be easily attributed to the ad. Although this method of measurement isn't holistic—it excludes the value of the incremental brand imagery and other effects from the commercial—it does provide a good estimate of the immediate value of the ad.

For B2B, small businesses, and businesses with a direct selling sales team, hard returns can be easily calculated for marketing actions, such as coupons, direct mail, outbound telemarketing, search engine marketing, and display advertising. Because these returns can be directly connected to an ad, sales can be easily predicted and therefore represent a relatively hard marketing investment.

Soft, less certain returns

On the other hand, there are many marketing investments that deliver soft, less certain returns. Depending on the business and the marketing action they can either fall into the soft or hard category. For example, a small brand without experience in mass media may consider television advertising soft. Larger, more experienced brands consider television much harder, because they have been measuring the response for many years. Oftentimes, whether an advertisement is soft or hard depends mostly on the level of investment spent to measure the impact of the advertisement, the type of business model and sophistication of the marketing infrastructure.

For B2B and companies selling through a sales force, webinars and trade shows/conferences can be considered soft, because they are one element of the overall consumer purchase process. These types of marketing activities are important, but often only work when combined with many other marketing and selling activities. It can be challenging to attribute the conversions to these actions, which combine to deliver the final conversion. Larger B2B marketers have gone to a point-scoring system, where each marketing action is given a certain number of points. These points are then tracked to determine the marketing actions with the highest number of points, which are credited with the conversion.

For B2B (for example enterprise-level high tech software sales), where the company and the customer generally require a lot of detailed and ongoing pre-sales communications, the entire contribution from marketing is often considered soft. Although the sales team believes they deserve all the credit for sales and therefore dismisses the value of marketing, they also don't want to see the marketing budget cut because they do believe marketing helps them convert deals faster and at a higher value with a higher win rate.

For consumer marketers, softer media channels include marketing channels such as sponsorships and product placements. The effectiveness of these media channels can be measured; however, in some cases, the cost of the data and measurement process relative to the investment in the sponsorship can be exorbitant. Even with the measurement data, there may be a lot of uncertainty in the exactitude of the success measurement.

For the marketing machine to function, it is critical to nevertheless determine the analytics for all types of marketing activities, especially the softer media channels. Most importantly, the marketing team must focus their efforts on:

1. the media channels where the investments are the greatest, and
2. the media channels that are believed to be the most impactful.

It's important to understand the most impactful media channels, as well as the most expensive (i.e., as a percentage of the overall working media budget), in order to build an effective marketing machine. For example, an email campaign may be very inexpensive, yet very impactful, compared with a television commercial, but both of them are important to understand in terms of their ability to deliver revenue.

The contribution from just about every media channel can be measured or modeled through a number of different methods. Prioritizing the measurement first by the level of investment (for example, the top media channels representing 80 to 90 percent of the marketing budget) is the first step to generating high overall marketing ROI. Next, because these are often more challenging to measure, determining the contribution of what are estimated to be the most impactful, low-investment media channels can lead to a further increase in overall marketing ROI. Email is an example of a high-impact, low-cost working media channel. Lastly, measuring the remaining media channels is still important, and will help to balance out the entire working media investment activities.

Baseline

Baseline is defined as the level of sales if there is no advertising. For example, advertising may cease for a few months for many reasons, but because the product is on the shelf, it is still purchased. Plus, because the consumer has used the brand in the past and has a connection with the brand, the product continues to be repurchased. It is this level of sales that is often defined as baseline. However, even though no advertising is being undertaken, the baseline may not be constant. Typically, if advertising is discontinued, the baseline begins to decay. Over a long period of time without any advertising, it would be expected to decay down to zero.

Baseline comprises three primary components:

1. The value of the brand
2. The impact of external factors
3. Competitive advertising

Promotional activation

Especially in Asia, many brands are now investing in jersey sponsorships in soccer. These sponsorships help to associate the winning team with the brand, but they don't necessarily drive consumers to purchase now. For example, Delta Airlines purchased the Leicestershire Jersey sponsorship, but they must also activate that sponsorship through in-game offers of Delta-branded SkyMiles and SkyMiles credit cards, or announcements of the addition of new destination cities.

As the value of the brand increases, the value of the baseline also increases. As the brand discontinues its advertising, the brand value decreases, leading to a decrease in the baseline. If the competition advertises, sales can go up or down. If sales are dependent on the economy or the weather, then these can lead to increases in the baseline. These influences also make up a portion of the true baseline. For a marketing machine to be accurate, it is critical that the marketing team understand the level of baseline and its decay and growth drivers; these will be critical inputs in determining the required level of incremental working media to achieve the overall sales plan in the face of growing or declining brand value, unpredictable competitive advertising, or unforeseen channel or external factors.

Dependent media channels (external factors)

Many media channels have non-marketing dependencies. Some media channels, if not all, are dependent on various external factors such as the economy or the seasons. Advertising in the summer for swimwear will be much more effective than the same advertising in the winter. It's imperative to understand these dependencies in order to build an effective media plan that meets the seasonal sales requirements of the business. Using a summer media success factor for the winter will definitely lead to incorrect measurements in the wrong season and inaccuracies in the marketing model. Either the sales plan for the slow season needs to be adjusted down, or the high season needs to be adjusted up, or both.

Optimizing media period by period

Seasonality can have interesting effects on marketing effectiveness. In many industries, media is less effective in certain quarters and more effective in others. For example, with certain types of insurance, media is less effective in Q1 than it is in the other three quarters. To deliver the most effective media, the company should only spend media where and when the media can deliver the most revenue. For certain types of insurance, this would mean spending little in Q1 and allocating that money to Q2 through Q4. But this would mean that revenue would be significantly lower in Q1, yet much higher in Q2 through Q4. This may be the best way to allocate media investments, but it would also mean that the investors would have to be informed that this is the new strategy. That continued quarter over quarter growth would not be delivered in the first quarter. On the other hand, if continued growth through each quarter was required, this would mean that the company would have to spend even more in Q1 in order to make up for the revenue shortfall due to the seasonality that it is fighting against. This would mean that, overall, the media effectiveness would decline significantly, because the company needed to overspend in the first quarter when media was the least effective.

Halo media

Some media works significantly better when combined together with other media. A branded sponsorship of a football game may build awareness, but if it is activated with in-game "act now" messages, then both the sponsorship and the promotional messages are more impactful. In fact, the synergy or halo value typically means that the returns from the combined media campaign are significantly higher than the sum of the returns for each of the media channels had they been executed separately.

Some modeling methods struggle with the measurement of the halo effect. Marketing analysts must take care when building a marketing model to use a method that can easily incorporate these effects. Most marketers build integrated marketing campaigns where the halo effect is counted on. If the modeling method can't properly handle these halo effects, it will provide erroneous answers when used in the marketing machine.

Predicting media impact

A marketing machine's primary goal is to be able to systematically deliver sales based on the planned and executed marketing investment. One of the challenges of that prediction is to determine the relative value of a creative concept. For example, what is the effectiveness of a new "polar bear" ad for Coca Cola?[37] Will it be 10% better than last year—or 25% worse?

Promotional: Coca-Cola Polar Bear

In order for the marketing machine to support the corporate decision-making, this relative difference must be known and any potential variations in the effectiveness must be planned for. There are a number of testing methods that can help to determine the potential effectiveness of a soon-to-be

---

[37] Coca-Cola Polar Bear Commercial: https://www.youtube.com/ watch?v=S2nBBMbjS8w, October 2016.

aired creative execution. For example, the Millward Brown Link test[38] can be used as a good indicator of future success compared with past creative concepts. Based on the results of a Link test, the relative impact of the new media campaign with the new creative can now be predicted with reasonable accuracy. With a marketing machine in place, the estimated sales levels can be simulated given the quality of the new creative concept in order to determine the level of media necessary to drive the sales plan.

The cost of measurement versus the cost of the media

For many companies, especially smaller companies, the cost to accurately measure a media activity can be extremely high. In these cases, marketers can potentially develop proxies for media success or they must find inexpensive ways to measure the media channel's effectiveness in order to help move the company along the path of an effective marketing machine. Even if the measurement methodology can only provide directional answers, it is critical to begin the measurement regimen in order to gain valuable insights for future advertising investments.

The marketing reserve

As explained in previous chapters, the marketing reserve is typically set at 15% to 20% of the monthly budget, or it is based on the potential expected variability or uncertainty in the overall market. If the softer part of the budget is proportionately larger than the harder part, the marketing reserve should be higher. If the competitive environment is especially dynamic (e.g., a new competitive launch is expected), the reserve should be higher. Or, if there is a lot of variability expected in external factors, the reserve should be higher. The purpose is to make certain that, in the face of uncertainty, the sales plan can be achieved without having to go back to obtain drawn-out marketing investment approvals, or worse yet, miss the numbers altogether and have to come back with an explanation.

---

[38] Millward Brown: https://www.millwardbrowndigital.com/blog-mobile-mantra/, September 2016.

Marketing experimentation

In the previous chapter, we mentioned that marketers also need money set aside for experimentation and taking advantage of promotional opportunities that might arise. We've seen the experimental budget be as high as 3% of the overall working media budget. In this way, marketers have the opportunity to run experiments without the necessity of full accountability. Nevertheless, a marketer must still include strong measurement in every experiment in order to make certain it can be a viable and positive alternative for the future if and when it is proven to be able to contribute great results.

Budgeting for price promotions

Price promotions are often run for stable mature brands to bring attention back to the brand. If the category is highly promotion-driven, price promotions are simply part of doing business in the category. The orange juice category was well-known for their price promotions; every single day products could be purchased by BOGO (Buy One Get One) or some other combination of offers. Consumers were so well trained to expect promotions in the category that they wouldn't purchase in the category until the next promotion became available. In essence, marketing was offering a lower price without actually changing the unpromoted MSRP (Manufacturers Suggested Retail Price).

Price promotions and coupons are also valuable in driving trials. Some major consumer package good (CPG) brands will drop hundreds of millions of coupons to spur trial when they launch a new brand into a category. These too need to be tracked and assigned to a line item within the marketing budget.

Price promotions are often captured as simply charges against revenue. Marketers are responsible for these costs; they need to have a budget line item to account for product sales purchased on promotion. That calculation needs to be part of their overall marketing mix when assembling their media and marketing plans.

Budgeting for packaging design changes

When making packaging design changes, there are two cost elements: the set-up costs, which are generally considered fixed, and the variable costs, which may raise or lower the production cost of the unit. These also must be considered part of the media mix.

Set-up costs

Typically, the brand is responsible for the set-up costs for packaging changes. These can include new tooling and dyes, design expenses, and potentially machine downtime to re-tool machines on the production line.

Variable costs

On the other hand, variable costs are built into the cost of the product and don't show up in the marketing budget, yet they are clearly an investment in the marketing mix to improve the position of the product on the shelf or in the minds of the consumer. If the packaging change was meant to spur sales, then if, for example, the new package costs an additional 1 cent per unit, this is an expense that needs to be borne by the marketing mix.

For a fully functional marketing machine, both types of costs must be captured, tracked, and attributed back to the marketing team. The redesigned, more expensive package represents a media message source, just like any other signage or advertising media channel.

Non-working marketing expenses and the marketing machine

As discussed above, non-working marketing expenses are everything other than the delivery of messages to the market. These are non-variable costs. They remain fixed regardless of whether the working media is scaled up or scaled down. Typical costs here include office space, personnel, computers, and other fixed investments to run the business of marketing.

The marketing machine is made up of a combination of people, process and technology. The people are the members of the marketing team, including the agency and other third-party vendors providing data and research. The process is the detailed rolling planning and execution cycle broadly described as execution, tracking, simulation, and planning. Marketing machine methodology and technology, partially made up of marketing IT, includes many different software tools and applications that support these highly valuable processes.

Market research, marketing data, and technology infrastructure make up a piece of the non-working media budget. Both are critical to a successful marketing machine. The more data, the better the consumer or distribution channel is understood. Through valid research, insights can be transformed into useful information to support improved marketing decision making.

If they aren't aligned with the marketing machine in one of the above categories, other costs in the marketing function are most likely superfluous and should be reduced or eliminated. If the expense can help to drive more sales, then it should be scrutinized to fit in the marketing machine. If not, it should be eliminated.

Sales and marketing budgets

Setting the overall sales and marketing budget should be easy. The shareholders and the C-Suite negotiate the top-line sales number and the top-line operating margins for the year. Each of these represent the level of growth expected overall and are based on what the shareholders want to see to validate their investments in the company, given the risk and reward opportunities of that investment. With a marketing machine in place, once these top-line numbers have been established, the company can determine the level of marketing investments required to meet those sales and profit levels.

Now comes the hard part. The split between the marketing (media and non-working marketing) and the sales budgets needs to be determined. Because the sales function is essentially a messaging function with the added capability to take the order, the marketing machine should be able to make the optimal allocation of budget between investments in marketing and investments in sales. At the conceptual level this is true. (As used in this instance, marketing is defined as the optimal delivery of messages to the market to effectuate the most sales at least cost and risk.)

At the political level, this is more challenging. The sales and marketing teams are typically set as equals in the budgeting process. A loss in investment in one group is seen as a loss of political power in the organization, regardless of whether or not it is the best use of funds. If the marketing budget goes up, the sales budget usually goes down a corresponding amount. During the transition from a non-marketing machine environment to a marketing machine, both departments are loath to relinquish any of their budgets and staff in favor of the other department. Sales uses last-touch attribution to justify its ability to deliver revenue from each member of the sales team. "I sold that" is the mantra coming from the sales team. On the other hand, marketing uses a more sophisticated approach to model the effectiveness of media touchpoints, but often does not include the investments and activities in sales.

Only when both sales and marketing are fully modeled can a true marketing machine be implemented. The marketing machine must include the investments made to deliver *all* messages received by the consumer, whether originating from traditional media or from sales.

Sales management overheads

Just as there are non-working marketing expenses, so too, are there non-working sales overheads. These are typically made up of the management team, office and equipment, training, and sales automation software (Customer Relationship Management and Sales Force Automation). For larger sales teams, the management costs are also related to the span of control[39] and should be identified as variables falling under the "working sales" costs. As an example, if there are 100 salespersons on the sales team, then with a span of control of 7, there would be about 14 or 15 managers. If the company decided to add 10 more salespersons, the company would also have to hire at least 1 additional manager if the span of control was to remain at 7.

Sales team investments

Most sales compensation plans have several components to them:

1. Base salary
2. Commissions
3. Performance bonuses and recognition prizes

---

[39] Span of control is defined as the number of direct reports a manager manages.

In addition, there are often expenses related to their activities, such as travel and other out-of-pocket expenses.

Depending on the size of the sales team, these costs represent the working sales cost and generally can be considered as a variable investment to increase sales. The more salespersons, the higher the expected revenue. The higher the level of commissions, the more product the salesperson sells. The higher the bonuses, the more the salesperson sells.

Sales activity tracking and data accuracy

Salespersons deliver messages to the consumer (and to the channel). These messages are represented as sales activities. They can be inbound calls, outbound calls, face-to-face visits, meetings at trade shows, and many other types of activities. For an inbound sales team, tracking the number and length of a call can be relatively easily accomplished through a call system and augmented by manual entries. Face-to-face metrics are more challenging. They rely on the self-reporting of the sales team, which sees the reporting function as a burden as well as an intrusion into their independence.

Determining the quality of these metrics and trying to consistently assign the prospect a status in the buying process can also be challenging. The buying process, often referred to as the purchase funnel (see figure), indicates how a prospective customer initially becomes aware. As a refresher, some of those prospective customers show interest and become a lead. Some of these leads move deeper into the purchase funnel and start gathering information and showing indications of a potential purchase in the short term. They become prospects. At some point these prospects make a purchase and convert and become customers. For some businesses, this process is relatively simple. For others, where the sales cycle stretches over many months and there are many interlocutors involved, this process can be quite complex.

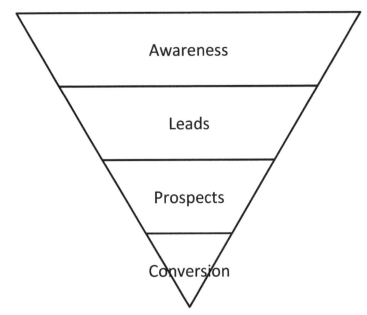

Figure 7: The B2B Purchase Funnel

Accurately and consistently tracking the customer as he or she moves through the purchase funnel is one of the most challenging activities when developing sales metrics and models. There are a number of ways to accomplish this tracking. SiriusDecisions, Marketo, and others provide great tools to manage and track this process.

Modeling

Modeling is a critical component of the marketing machine. There are three primary components to the full implementation of the modeling elements in a marketing machine. The figure below shows the interrelationships between the model types:

1. Traditional media – typically modeled in a marketing mix model
2. Digital media – typically modeled using attribution modeling
3. Sales – typically modeled using sales modeling

The all-encompassing resulting model would also be called a marketing mix model, even though a marketing mix model is sometimes limited in scope to cover just the marketing media channels and not necessarily the sales and other channels.

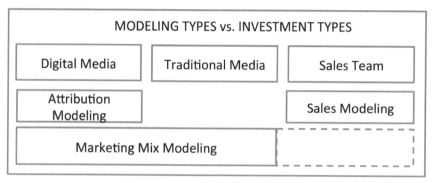

Figure 8: Modeling Types versus Investment Types

For many organizations modeling sales investments can be challenging; the data is often difficult to capture in an accurate fashion. Much of the sales activities are manual, and relying on individuals to capture these processes leaves a lot of room for interpretation. Data entries can be forgotten and/or made erroneously. Salespersons often dispute the value of the data and the best sales team members may simply refuse to participate. Without accurate data, it is difficult to build an accurate model, and because the data is challenged, the validity and accuracy of the sales model results are often disputed. Also, because the sales team provides both highly valuable messages and takes the order, the order-taking function and related costs must be removed from the model in order to determine a true comparison between returns on sales investments versus returns on marketing investments.

The communication and negotiation inherent in balancing the budget between marketing and sales will grow the marketing machine in two ways. First, the modeling and measuring will improve because a new priority will be placed on accurate figures as each department jostles for appreciation. More importantly, by working as a cohesive unit, the sales and marketing teams will be in a better position to begin working together to build the future.

Building the Future

When it comes to projecting the future, there are four dimensions to include in the development of a successful marketing plan:

1. Competitive actions
2. Channel factors
3. External factors
4. Reducing risk

If we knew exactly what the competition were about to do and how channel and external trends were going to unfold, we could easily predict the future. Channel and external factors are typically easier to predict. Unfortunately, the most challenging predictions of the future are the estimates of competitive actions in the marketplace:

- Are they going to launch a new product?
- Are they going to launch a great new creative advertising campaign?
- Are they going to change their pricing policy?
- Are they going to overhaul their distribution strategy?

All these dimensions contribute to uncertainty in determining how the future will unfold. In addition, reasonable estimates as to a competitor's next actions can be impacted by other structural changes in the competition. For example, senior level personnel changes may change a competitor's philosophy in how they approach the market, disturbing our ability to project how they will act in the future in the marketplace. Some of their actions may affect us or another specific competitor directly; others affect the whole marketplace, but only slightly touch each individual competitor. Nevertheless, understanding how these actions influence the market and our own sales is critical to building a functional and accurate marketing machine.

To develop a marketing machine, we not only need to understand the impact of our actions on consumer behavior, we also need to understand the impact of competitive actions, not to mention the impact of channel and external factors on each of the competitors and on the category size overall.

Competitive actions

Competitive actions can take many forms. They can be relatively regular, yet vary in intensity. They can also be very irregular. In order to properly plan the future, we need to know what the competition can do and then adjust our plans accordingly to accommodate the potential impact of these actions. It is vital that we put together competitive scenarios of our best, most informed estimate of their possible actions based on what they've done in the past and what we believe they might do in the future. We've found that future competitive actions can often be predicted with varying levels of accuracy. Lastly, total advertising volume in a category can expand the category size. If a competitor makes a significant change in advertising level, this can lead to a change in the overall level of activity and volume in the category which can have a positive or negative effect on our sales. For example, in the personal hygiene category, in one of the categories we've worked in, we've found that about half of the manufacturers advertise with a similar seasonal pattern year over year. We've also reviewed their temporary price reduction strategy and there seemed to be no discernible pattern whatsoever among all the vendors analyzed.

Repetitive and seasonal

We've found many competitors to be repetitive in what they do year over year. Although no one can say for certain what a competitor will do, we can with reasonable certainty make informed guesses that can be corrected and adjusted as the year unfolds. For example, Competitor A may always begin their mass marketing campaign in March and extend it 4 months through June. This pattern may have held over the past 3 years, meaning it is a good estimate that it will continue into the future. This competitor A generally seems to spend about $12m per year, but with an increasing budget growth of 6.5%. The company seems to be shifting their budgets toward digital with their digital spending beginning strong in the beginning of the month and ending near the end of the month possibly due to their budgets running out.

There are variants on these predictable advertisements; mass media campaigns may begin at different times during the year, but with roughly the same flighting, except shifted forward or backward. Once the campaign begins, it always seems to last 4 months.

Chaotic, totally unpredictable

Competitor B has a very unpredictable media execution plan. Every year the media flighting throughout the year seems completely chaotic. It never begins at the same time of year and its flighting, campaign length, and budget seem to vary each time. Most times these campaigns are tied to a major launch, but sometimes they're not. They seem to be totally random. These kinds of companies are the most challenging to predict. Marketers simply need to take a best guess of the potential worst case and best case and use those estimates in their planning process. In this way, marketers can develop an upper and lower bound of competitor B's influence on their own success in order to build and optimize potential plans to succeed in the face of this uncertainty.

This same process needs to be repeated for the major competitors' media channels, price actions, in-store promotions, and distribution levels in order to gather a full picture of how a competitor's actions can impinge on our success.

Channel factors

Channel factors include trends and possible disruptions that take place in the distribution channel.

Shifts in channel purchasing

Especially in Asia and Africa, there is a shift of consumer purchasing from traditional trade to modern trade. Modern trade channels, made up of numerous stores with sophisticated internal structures and processes, have operating cost advantages and are quickly changing the landscape of where consumers purchase many products. This is exacerbated by the ongoing shift from purchasing products in brick and mortar stores to online e-commerce sites. Major retailers have been developing their online ordering processes and delivery mechanisms so that they can provide a high-quality, seamless customer experience throughout the customer purchase process, whether online or in brick-and-mortar stores.

Step changes in retail

In addition to the trending changes mentioned above, the retail channel is going through significant upheaval regarding the overall success of specific retail chains. In the worst case, retailers are going out of business, causing step changes in their impact on the fortunes of the brand and in consumer purchase behavior. The loss of a valuable distribution channel partner can have significant deleterious effects on the future of a brand dependent on that channel.

External factors

External factors can also have a strong influence on the growth of the category overall, or on the growth of specific competitors in the category. A category can grow or decline significantly due to the effect of a single external factor. External factors can include effects of the weather, seasonality, technological innovation, and government regulation. External factors come in many flavors, but when projecting the future, we need to consider the following:

Trends

Trends are the simplest to project into the future. For example, the market has been growing at 4% per year and it is expected that it will continue to grow at that rate. The trend may change slightly, increasing to 5% or decreasing to 3%, but it may be generally expected to continue on an upward path. Economic growth and other effects typically have a smooth trending impact on overall category size.

Step effects

Government regulations typically have a step impact on a complete category. A step effect external factor has a one-time impact on the level of demand in the category. However, with government regulations and other step effects, we know both that they will occur and when they will be put into effect. We also know that once they take place they have a one-time, sometimes positive, sometimes negative, impact on the overall size of the market.

Risk reduction

Reducing risk doesn't mean that we simply outspend the competition at every turn. Unfortunately, marketing doesn't have unlimited resources to do that. Marketers must be smart in how plans are developed and executed to reduce risk. Risk falls into many categories:

1. Measurement risk
2. Model accuracy risk
3. Failure-to-imagine risk
4. Competitive action risk
5. Consumer behavior risk
6. Channel factor risk
7. External factor risk

The first three risks are to a large extent under our control. The last four are outside of our control but can be mitigated in a number of ways.

Measurement risk

Measurement risk can be mitigated by making certain the most important data is captured and tracked and properly warehoused. No marketer can measure everything, but by measuring the right things with the right level of granularity and timeliness this risk can be reduced. The right things generally follow measurements defined in the 4P3CEIF data framework provided on page 31 and can deliver the best results and reduced risk. Structuring the measurements to track what is occurring at the consumer level will do the most to mitigate measurement risk.

Change is the new constant

Although this sounds like a tired slogan, it has some interesting implications for the technological world we live in. If change is constant, then we can set our watch to it and plan for it. If change is constant, then what we need to look out for is the lack of change.

Today, some would even say that change is accelerating. We are experiencing new things at an ever-faster rate. New iPhones are coming to market faster and faster with dizzying arrays of new features and capabilities. I've found that most of the features aren't even used by most of the people that own them. We now have so much capability at our fingertips that we don't even need nor have the time to know everything that has changed.

Model accuracy risk

Model accuracy risk is dependent on the accuracy of the model. If the model is continually updated, tested, and revalidated, then this risk will tend to decrease as time goes on. With each iteration and refinement, a model can be challenged with new future scenarios and improved to capture more and more potential scenarios that might face the company. Over time, the model will continue to grow and learn and will become more accurate/less risky.

Modeling inaccuracy also occurs when some data is available on a weekly basis, some on a monthly basis, and some on a quarterly basis. Depending on the modeling method, these period-based measurement challenges can lead to inaccuracies that may not be possible to entirely overcome.

Failure-to-imagine risk

Many companies become complacent in their success, resulting in one or more years of setbacks following a long string of success. Many times, the culprit is simply the failure to imagine. The complacency in the team's thinking comes when the team isn't challenged as hard as it should be. If there isn't a constant rivalry or if the management team doesn't stress the company, then they become complacent and miss signals that might otherwise have been noticed and incorporated into their thinking. Marketers must never fail to imagine.

Competitive risk

Guessing what the competition is up to is an art that can be supported by science. Using the right methods, we can learn their ways and potentially deduce how the organization thinks. Although there are often non-compete agreements for top management, knowledge of the inner workings of organizations travels past the exit door whenever any employee leaves one company and begins working at the competition. Public trade presentations, press releases, and just general tracking can provide good insight as to what is going on and how it can be assembled into an understanding of their next actions.

The exact details can only be estimated, but there are nevertheless a few methods to improve the modeling of their impact. Although we don't know the exact level of media budget, we can estimate the upper and lower limit with reasonable certainty. With that in mind, we can test these two limits. Then we can set an expected value to be able to model its impact on our sales. As time unfolds we can update our guesses with the latest data to continue to fine tune our knowledge of their marketing's impact on our sales and adjust our marketing accordingly. There are many other methods that can be employed, but this is one of the best, especially when there is a clear and close rivalry between our and their brand.

In larger markets where there are many near-equal brands, the direct impact of one competitor on another is much less, so it is perhaps only the general impact that is important to track and react to.

Consumer behavior risk

In some ways, consumer behavior is a constant; in others, it can change very quickly. Consumer decision-making is generally quite stable. They have a need or want, they become aware, they gather information, they build preferences, they make comparisons, they make a purchase, and then they tell others. What is changing is the way consumers move through the first few stages of the purchase process described above. With near-perfect, instantaneous information at the consumers' fingertips through their mobile devices, the time to decision has now collapsed and the clarity with which they make decisions has become crystal. In addition, the speed and ability to tell others has now accelerated.

With shipping costs and returns options for many products being significantly reduced, the risk of making a bad purchase is also reduced. This allows smaller non-branded solutions to more easily join the consumer's consideration set.

These trends don't necessarily add risk. As marketers, we should already have incorporated these trends into our decision-making and into our modeling. What is more important as it relates to consumer risk is whether there is a change in the described consumer purchase decision behavior. Changes take place when there are shocks to the system. Shocks can include the 9-11 terrorist attack on the NY World Trade Center, a sudden instability in the markets (such as the Brexit vote in the U.K.), or any other shock that would cause consumer spending patterns to change. These are the risks that we need to be ready for and have built into our models. Often in these kinds of cases, purchase decisions are pushed out a few months, consumers temporarily leave the category, or their price elasticity changes to where they are more likely to choose the lower cost item and disregard the emotional value of the premium brand. It is the understanding of these kinds of shocks to the system that we need to have at the ready so that we can quickly enter them into our planning and modeling if these root causes occur.

If we know what the effect of these kinds of root causes can be, we can have backup marketing plans at the ready if and when they occur.

Channel factor risk

If there are no dynamics in the channel, then there is little risk in this dimension. Unfortunately, in most countries the channel structures are rapidly changing. Mom-and-Pop stores are being replaced by modern trade. Brick-and-mortar shopping is being replaced by online shopping. Channel players are going bankrupt and new formats and new concepts are being developed. The channel is often not as stable as we'd like; major disruptions in the channel can impact how and where a consumer gathers information, goes shopping, and makes a purchase. These dynamics and the related uncertainties can be built into the modeling and a best/worst/expected–case scenarios set can be built and analyzed.

External factor risk

External factor risks are partially covered in the above discussion on consumer behavior risk, but there are other external factors, such as seasonal variations, that provide uncertainty in the modeling process week to week and month to month. An especially cold winter may lead to higher natural gas consumption in most of the U.S., reducing the need for strong advertising, or a particularly rainy summer may reduce the demand for new sets of golf clubs. These kinds of factors don't necessarily deal with changing consumer behavior. Instead, we are seeing expected behavior based on the presence of these external factors. Marketers simply need to look at best, worst, and expected cases for each of these factors and determine what the potential impact might be. If necessary, further detail can be developed through a more granular scenario definition.

Analyzing risk versus outcomes

Risk profiles represent the level of risk of a particular marketing plan across a set of scenarios. Scenarios represent sets of potential futures. Each scenario represents a possible future with some mix of estimated competitive marketing plans, channel actions, and external factors against which various marketing plans are run. To determine the risk profile, each of the marketing plans are run against each of the possible scenarios and outcomes are determined. Based on expectations and the modeled outcomes, marketers can determine the level of impact each of the competitors, channel factors, or external factors has on the outcome. These varying outcomes represent the level of risk in the marketing plans, providing a risk profile against which the best marketing plans can be chosen.

At any point in time there are an infinite number of potential futures. Not only can the plans be changed by the level of estimated competitive spend, but also by its timing. In a complex category with many major competitors (each with different expectations along their product, price, and promotion dimensions), it's easy to see that there are many different potential futures. To handle this level of complexity, a number of methods can be applied to determine the level of risk in a particular best-case marketing plan.

Best/Worst/Expected variable sets

In most cases, as we've explained, three scenarios can be tested for a single variable set: What is the best case (for us), what is the most likely or best guess, and what is the worst case (for us). In each of these cases, we would run a scenario to determine the simulated outcome to determine whether it will have a strong or weak adverse effect on our sales volume. If there is a strong influence on our outcomes, then we would need to investigate further. If there is a weak impact on our outcomes, then it may suffice to look elsewhere for potential sources of larger uncertainty (where uncertainty is synonymous with risk) due to the unknowns in the marketplace.

Monte Carlo simulation sets

In many instances of scenario simulation, there are simply far too many combinations of variables to simulate all combinations in a reasonable amount of time for a reasonable amount of cost and effort. In this case, a simplification can be built where random sets of variables can be chosen for competitive actions, channel factors, and external factors in order to determine a set of simulated outcomes that can be used to make estimates for Best/Worst/Expected cases. Similarly, a random set of marketing plans can also be developed based on random combinations of the company's own marketing inputs (media, price, distribution, and product). Against each of these scenarios, the random set of marketing plans can be run to find which plans perform best and worst. The difference in outcomes represents the risk profile of the given marketing plan given an uncertain future. The best-performing plans represent a near-optimal marketing plan within some error range (of the actual optimal marketing plan). This is one possible route to searching for a close and good estimate of the best marketing plan and the uncertainty and risk associated with its output. The larger the size of the random sample, the closer the best/worst outcome of the Monte Carlo simulations will be to the actual best/worst simulation. At some point during the random simulations, the best/worst will be asymptotically reached where the level of increase in the best will be insignificant against unknowns elsewhere in the simulation and modeling process.

Linear search algorithm

Marketers can also search in a linear way, first determining which variables have the most and least influence for a given scenario. Once these are known, the best marketing plan is built by first determining the diminishing returns for the best variable, then for the next best, and so on until a final "best" marketing mix is found for a given scenario. This can be repeated against a random set of competitive plans, channel factors, and external factors to estimate the level of risk and uncertainty with this "best" marketing plan. Further refinements to the plan can be made based on testing key assumptions against the best-, expected-, and worst-case outcomes until a desired outcome has been found that presents the best tradeoff between uncertainty in outcomes and overall outcome.

There are many other methods to determine the potential uncertainty in our lack of knowledge of the future that are well beyond the scope of this book. For more on predicting competitor behavior, check out *Learning from the Future* by Randall and Fahey[40], as well as this *Harvard Business Review* article, "Predicting Your Competitor's Reaction" by Kevin Coyne and John Horn from April 2009[41].

---

[40] Learning from the Future: Competitive Foresight Scenarios. Oct 1997. Robert M. Randall and Liam Fahey

[41] https://hbr.org/2009/04/predicting-your-competitors-reaction, August 2017.

Chapter **11**

Building a Marketing Machine

Building a marketing machine is no simple task. It requires inputs from several critical departments, including IT, marketing, sales, and accounting. The marketing machine needs several different layers of analytics, with the most important being the ongoing marketing optimization.

Marketing analytics in a marketing machine

There are four levels to the marketing analytics function encompassed in a marketing machine:

1. **Descriptive** – Most important when looking at past and current data is simply to determine what happened and what is happening. Knowing the facts and viewing them through a consistent lens is the first part of being able to diagnose various situations—and being able to make the right decisions to determine what will happen and how the organization can best respond.

2. **Diagnostic** – Once what happened and what is happening has been determined, the organization can start to understand the causes behind specific situations. For example, why are sales declining in traditional trade? Or, how effective is the new price promotion offered by our biggest competitor?

3. **Predictive** – Once we understand what seems to be the root causes of specific situations found in the marketplace, the organization can start to predict the consequences of these situations moving forward. What could be the worst case and what could be the best case? How would those change with a given response?

4. **Optimized** – Lastly, we need to respond to these actions to mitigate any prospective losses and plan how to achieve our corporate targets. We need to develop a new or modified plan for how to get back on track or grow even faster. We need to optimize our marketing plans with the new scenario given the new competitive, channel, or external factors.

Implementation process

The following steps represent the best plan for a successful implementation of a marketing machine:

1. **Scope refinement** – Making certain the project plan is well and fully defined is critical to the success of any project. The scope refinement must include a reiteration of the objectives, along with sub-objectives and milestone definitions, each with potential timeframes. The objective of building a marketing machine is to build a clear connection between marketing activities and the achievement of the corporate revenue plan. The scope must also include objectives regarding the value associated with current data sets, as well as possible future datasets and what they could mean to future refinements of a marketing machine. It must identify key individuals and departments that will be affected by the marketing machine. Lastly, it must review current weaknesses in the connections within the marketing (and selling) teams as well as connections with the rest of the company.

2. **Market overview and business situation understanding** – Critical to the implementation of the marketing machine is understanding the marketplace and the consumers, competition, and channel and external factors driving the marketplace. This will help to make certain that critical dimensions of how consumers make purchase decisions and how key influences impact those decisions are included. This knowledge leads to understanding how current and future data streams can be added and implemented in the marketing machine.

3. **Project team identification** – Critical members of the team need to be determined and assigned roles in the project. This includes the

requisite members from the marketing team, marketing analytics, market research, IT, and legal. For any project of this nature, executive support is critical to make certain resources and priorities are properly set. This must be set out clearly from the start.

4. **Data discovery** – Because the marketing machine relies on solid and timely sources of consumer, channel, and competitive data, the current sources of data must be understood to discover how they can be used to drive the building of the machine. This also needs to include the costs of the data sources, of the manual or automated processing (if any), as well as of any potential future data sources that may add to the value and accuracy of the machine. It needs to include a calendar of periodic data updates so that its connection into the workflow can be properly planned. Data must now be tested and vetted for completeness and accuracy.

5. **Infrastructure discovery** – In this step, the current IT, legal, and personnel infrastructure is analyzed and audited to understand any potential requirements for the handling of data, the speed of data access, and the technical and marketing understanding of the affected personnel. In this way, the requisite training can be designed and put in place for the individuals who will be implementing the marketing machine.

6. **Workflow training** – Here the affected personnel in the previous step are trained on the top-level objectives of the marketing machine, the methodologies underlying the marketing machine, and how to operate it and obtain the best results. It is best to provide training before, during, and after implementation of the machine so that the requisite buy-in is in place.

7. **Marketing machine technical installation** – The installation of the machine is a straightforward yet technical activity. The team must provide the various links and access controls into various internal and external datasets.

8. **Model building** – The marketing machine is based on a model that needs to be built considering the data and the market structure, then tuned to fit the market. Once the model is in place, initial strategic recommendations can be made, with the goal to have these ultimately flow into the rolling planning process.

9. **Model sign-off** – The rolling marketing machine process cannot move forward until the model is signed off and approved. This is critical to make certain that the model has incorporated all pertinent data, the fits are within standards, and the model is predictive.

10. **Building the first future** – Building the first future is the most difficult of all the steps in the implementation process. Because there is often general risk aversion about projecting into the future, the project team must work to tease out potential futures. We've found there is more information in the minds of the marketing team than they realize. Initial estimates can vary widely from what is found in the market. As time moves forward, this first future will be refined to where there are fewer and fewer surprises. The known knowns get larger and more accurate, the known unknowns get more defined, and the unknown unknowns offer fewer surprises.

11. **Building and testing scenarios/optimizing the marketing plan** – Once the first future is built, variations on that future can be developed based on uncertainties within the marketing plan. Testing the model and optimizing the marketing plan against these scenarios can now begin. Risk assessments can be made based on the likelihoods of each of the scenarios and variations to the marketing plan can be developed should the future unfold along one path versus another.

12. **Building response packages** – Testing various scenarios against very specific unknown, but highly probable, events allows the marketing team to build response packages. These packages represent a series of activities that can be executed to respond to a specific event. If—and when—an event takes place, the marketing team now only needs to adjust the package to be able to meet the specifics of the unfolding event. This saves significant time in the response timeline, builds confidence in the right response, and allows the team to explore more options to mitigate any adverse effects of the event.

13. **Initial process testing** – Once the model is in place, the first few rounds of periodic analysis and recommendation building must be run and scrutinized. This will generate confidence, not only in the model, but also in the process. Data and model validation processes

must be developed so that data anomalies can be avoided. Testing and validation of the process needs to be continually updated in order to build further confidence in the process and avoid any potential model or process inaccuracies.

14. **Re-assessing the future of the marketing machine** - A marketing machine must stay current with the market and be flexible enough to evolve as fast or faster than the rest of the competitors. The marketing machine team must always be on the lookout for new data sets and algorithms that can provide new options to improve ROI, the optimization process, and predictability. With a functioning marketing machine, the cost of the new data sets and algorithms can easily be weighed against their value to determine whether the investment in them will incrementally improve the overall marketing effectiveness of the organization. The team should meet quarterly and annually to assess the state of the data market and competitive, channel, and external factors to determine if there are new third-party data sets or algorithms—or if there are new opportunities to generate new primary data sources or analytic algorithms. In addition, the processes should continue to be evaluated for improvement and automation opportunities.

Building in flexibility

When critical processes are implemented to support business and marketing decision making, the marketing team must take care not to build in inflexibility. Just as the implementation of ERP systems have dealt major blows to the flexibility of an organization, a marketing machine may be perceived along the same lines. However, when implemented as discussed, this can and will be avoided. The planned periodic updating of data and the competitive situation lends itself to flexibility. Because the period can be down to the weekly level, the business can easily make quick decisions in order to be on top of the situation in the marketplace and respond with confidence and speed as necessary.

Partial/step-wise implementation

A marketing machine can be implemented all at once or in a few key steps. The above process takes the company to a full implementation, but for many companies, this may not be possible. Instead, a stepwise process may be more appropriate. For some small businesses and many B2B marketers, the investment to implement a full marketing machine may need to be spread over a few years. If this is the case, then marketers must define a few interim steps to build their marketing machines.

Here are a few initial steps that can help the marketing team begin to develop critical infrastructure for a marketing machine:

Data: Develop a data infrastructure of consumer purchase decision behavior

Using the consumer data framework described above as a reference, start to determine how to capture these data points on a weekly or monthly cycle and put them into a marketing warehouse. It is critical to capture data that tracks how consumers make purchase decisions. In the consumer package goods industry, this can mean capturing transaction data from the retail channel. In pharmaceuticals, it may mean capturing how physicians write prescriptions for specific drugs and how patients fulfill those prescriptions.

Interim metrics: Develop a measurement infrastructure

A measurement infrastructure should include accurate tracking of interim success metrics based on the consumer purchase funnel or, for B2B, steps in the lead generation process. Marketers should know for each media channel the impact major marketing investment channels and campaigns have at each of the major levels in the purchase funnel and/or the lead generation process. The measurements should start with the major investment items and then move to the progressively smaller and smaller marketing channels.

Use simple last-touch attribution or experimental design to build a culture of measurement, then work to develop accuracy and consistency in these measurements.

Financial success metrics: Begin measuring marketing effectiveness for the major marketing investment items

Select the top marketing investment channels (those representing 80% of the working media budget) and work to determine the ROMI factors for each of these channels. This will help prioritize where major investments should be made and how they can help achieve financial success. Make certain that the results are defined with a common, well-defined metric for success. Mixing success metrics for different media channels or areas of the business will only lead to confusion and failure of the marketing machine.

Simulator: Build and validate a media simulator

Build a simulator for the major media channels. Assuming that all else is equal—that is, pricing, distribution channels, product features, and product functionality—and that competitive, channel, and external factors don't change, build and test a simple, linear simulator to begin predicting future sales. Add in different competitive actions in order to determine their potential risks and provide levels of risk based on various potential futures.

Process: Build a periodic process to regularly incorporate simulation findings

Achieving the monthly and quarterly numbers is critical for the sales and marketing team. Regularly working through the process to review the current period's interim and success achievement is critical. You'll need the latest sales and marketing plans and the latest estimates of competitive, channel, and external factors in order to make the most well-informed projections of the immediate future prospects for the company.

There are many other potential ways to make a stepwise progression in implementing a marketing machine. Those listed above represent the key dimensions of a marketing machine: data, measuring effectiveness of interim and financial success factors, building a simulator, and implementing a periodic review process.

For the CEO

In this discussion, we define sales and marketing separately. Sales is technically a marketing channel with the added capability that it can take the order. Marketing is often thought of as different from sales; that is, marketing doesn't include the face-to-face, belly-to-belly selling function, but in reality, sales is another source of highly persuasive (and highly valuable) messages. This is not to diminish the value of the selling function, rather to make certain that we realize that marketing overall is the function of managing the message delivery across *all* channels so that customers/consumers can move down the purchase funnel more quickly, at lower cost and risk, to convert into a sale and later to advocate for the company. The selling function is just one method and one media channel to accomplish this critical activity.

Marketing machine design

Many times, businesses are limited in their growth prospects based on their preconceived notions of where their revenue comes from. Clearly the sales team is one of the most important assets in the company. The issue is how can marketing make the sales team more effective overall. In order to do that, we need to consider how the sales team fits in with the marketing equation (see sidebar). Is the sales function separate from marketing? Is marketing a sub-function to sales, or is sales a sub-function to marketing? These are at the root of the challenges facing many companies, especially in B2B and B2B2C.

Small businesses often begin their success with a strong sales structure. Start-up CEOs are extremely good at selling and their background is likely in sales or business development. Because of this they know how to build a sales plan, leverage their relationships, and meet a quota. They are, in essence, a one-person marketing machine. This capability works until they hire their first few salespersons and the machine either steps up to the next level or plateaus. The more salespersons they hire, the fewer and fewer incremental sales each new hire generates. This is a typical situation reflecting diminishing returns in a marketing channel. The issue for the business is how to make a leap in sales and marketing effectiveness. How can the business generate more sales overall with the same sales team?

In these smaller businesses, marketing is often perceived as the team responsible for putting together a handful of brochures and collateral materials, maintaining and updating the website, but not developing more leads and more business. This equation needs to be flipped upside-down; marketing needs to drive the process of moving customers/consumers down the purchase funnel. In essence, the sales team was originally performing this marketing function, but for smaller companies to move to the next level this process needs to be delegated to a less costly function that can focus on these specific challenges at a lower cost, still leaving the conversion to the sales team.

The goal of the new marketing function is to transform the sales organization into one that can deliver significantly more revenue for the same level of investment, or to allow the team to grow in a non-diminishing, more linear way. We need to return the sales team to being a marketing machine that can grow revenue, one where an incremental investment can deliver a known level of return in a predictable and accountable fashion.

Building an objectives-based (sales and) marketing plan

There are four dimensions to building an objectives-based marketing plan and budget. These include planning:

1. By customer or segment
2. By product
3. By distribution channel
4. By price

Other disaggregation dimensions exist, but the four listed above are the most prevalent and will be the focus in this section.

Each of these dimensions helps to put together a toolbox for the company to effectively invest critical resources in a predictable and accountable way. At the core of this planning methodology is to determine the level of sales for each level of investment—that is, to know the marketing ROI or Return on Marketing Investment (ROMI or mROMI). If we have these methods in hand and we fully understand them, then we can easily build the requisite sales and marketing budgets and plans. Sophisticated marketers build their marketing budgets and plans based on a combination of these dimensions.

Objectives-based budgeting by customer or segment

Every company has customers, consumers, or prospects in each of the following relationship categories. (Although the term "customer" is used in the following discussion, "segment" could be easily substituted). This method of marketing budgeting and planning is ideal for companies with one-to-one relationships with their customers; for example, telecommunications, financial services, B2B, and many others. The relationships include:

- Non-customers
- Former customers
- New customers
- Existing customers
- Advocating customers

The goal of marketing is to move customers (or segments) quickly and inexpensively from being non-customers to becoming a customer, then to becoming and staying a high-use customer and lastly, a brand advocate. Marketing does this in various ways. Marketing can structure their budgets along these categories in order to more appropriately build an effective budget and plan the actions required to support these movements.

Marketing needs to build its budget by identifying these key customer flows, determining the level of spend appropriate for each flow, and optimizing accordingly.

Winning new customers (or segments)

Winning new customers is generally known to be the most expensive type of marketing, but often it is also the most important to grow a business. Having current customers potentially churning by moving to the competition means that, without new customers, the company will decline and eventually fade away. Winning new customers may need to start with building awareness at the top of the funnel, then building purchase intent, and finally converting. Identifying the appropriate resources and metrics necessary to manage and accelerate this process is at the heart of customer acquisition strategies.

Upselling and cross-selling existing customers (or segments)

Once new customers make their first purchase with the company, it is up to marketing to push that customer to continue to purchase the same level (or more) of goods and services from the company. Ideally, based on the customer's needs, the company needs to move the customers to be at their maximum level of spend with the company. If their consumption starts to wane, marketing must step in to determine how to reinvigorate sales from existing customers.

Many customers purchase the same types of products from more than one source. This is especially true for B2B. They prefer to have second sources for products so they can balance their negotiating position between them. If the customer is purchasing from your company and the competition at the same time, it is up to marketing to help shift as many purchases away from the competition as possible.

Mitigating churn or attrition

The worst case for our existing customers is to have them stop consuming altogether, or to move their consumption over to the competition. This is called attrition or churn. Sometimes churn can be due to negative service incidents or better product offerings from the competition. In some cases, churn isn't exactly known. For banks, the consumer may keep their account open, but may stop using it. Activity goes to near zero.

With the right analytics, marketing can take specific actions to mitigate churn. Churn analytics analyzes how a company's customer touchpoints, such as marketing messages, customer service quality and even billing, can lead to higher or lower churn. By understanding the drivers of churn marketing message timing and content, as well as customer service, delivery and billing statements can be modified to mitigate this churn.

Moving customers (or segments) to advocacy

With the advent of social media, marketers can now assist and motivate their customers to spread the good news about their products. In the past, user groups would be set up so that a company's user community could be leveraged to provide input and feedback to the company and provide support and other valuable communications about the company's products between customers in a peer-to-peer fashion. Now social media performs a similar function but at a much higher scale. It is one goal of marketing to influence customers to provide strong advocacy to prospective and fellow customers to mitigate churn and to support the customer acquisition and customer support process.

The following case study of a B2B Telecommunications division highlights the impact of objectives-based marketing planning and budgeting.

B2B Telecommunications: New customer acquisition, churn and upselling

B2B Data communications for global corporations is a highly sales-intensive selling and marketing industry segment. Contracts are sold between the telecommunications company and their large corporate customers for specific sets of complex telecommunications and data communications services. These contracts typically last 36 months, although they can last longer. Often the costs of changing from one telecommunications provider to another are very high, so even though the contract has a fixed length, the likelihood of churn from one contract period to the next is very low. It may be on the order of 20% per contract. If the average contract revenue per month is $10,000, this means that each contract on average is worth $360,000 over the 3-year contract or $120,000 per year.

For the sake of simplicity, let's assume that the timing between expiring contracts is spread evenly across all 36 months. This means that every month, 1 out of the 36 contracts are up for renewal (2.8%). This also means that, barring some major aberration in service, the other non-expiring contracts will not terminate at that time. Because this is a contract business, then, every year only 33.3% of the revenue is potentially at risk. But if the churn rate is 20%, that actually means that only 6.7% is at risk and, based on past history, would have moved to the competition. 93.3% of the revenue is almost guaranteed. The company can do nothing in sales and marketing and 93.3% of the revenue will continue unabated!

In the table below, an example company has 500 customers, each generating $10,000 per month in revenue. That totals to $5,000,000 per month in total revenue and $60,000,000 per year. On average, the company generates 7.6 new customers per month; without churn, the company can grow from $60M to $66M in revenue within a year. At the end of the year with this monthly growth rate, the company has 549.6 customers and has grown at a rate of 18.3%.

	Jan	Feb	Mar		Oct	Nov	Dec	Totals/ Averages
Baseline no new customers	500.0	500.0	500.0	...	500.0	500.0	500.0	500.0
Baseline revenue	$5,000,000	$5,000,000	$5,000,000	...	$5,000,000	$5,000,000	$5,000,000	$60,000,000
New customers	7.6	7.6	7.6	...	7.6	7.6	7.6	91.7
Total customers	507.6	515.3	522.9	...	576.4	584.0	591.7	549.65
Revenue with growth	$5,076,389	$5,152,778	$5,229,167	...	$5,763,889	$5,840,278	$5,916,667	$65,958,333

Key Assumptions	
Average monthly revenue	$10,000
New customer growth rate	18.3%

With 20% churn per month among contracts coming up for renewal, the company requires another 6.7% (33.3) new customers in order to maintain the revenue at an even level. (See table below.)

NO GROWTH WITH CHURN	Jan	Feb	Mar		Oct	Nov	Dec	Totals/ Averages
Baseline no new customers	500.0	500.0	500.0	...	500.0	500.0	500.0	500.0
Customer w/ renew contract	13.9	13.9	13.9	...	13.9	13.9	13.9	13.9
Expected churn customers	2.8	2.8	2.8	...	2.8	2.8	2.8	2.8
New customers	2.8	2.8	2.8	...	2.8	2.8	2.8	33.3
Total customers	500.0	500.0	500.0	...	500.0	500.0	500.0	500.0
Revenue with growth	$4,999,972	$4,999,972	$4,999,972	...	$4,999,972	$4,999,972	$4,999,972	$59,999,667

Key Assumptions	
Average monthly revenue	$10,000
New customer growth rate	18.3%
Expected churn rate of renewers	20%
Renewal rate per month	2.8%
Replacement customer win rate	6.66%

Churn Analysis	
Average churn rate at 19%	1.39
Average churn rate at 20%	2.78
Revenue diff of churned customers (annual)	$166,333

In the table above, we are analyzing a company with 500 customers and a churn rate of 20% of those that are up for renewal each month. If 13.9 customers are up for renewal in a given month and 20% of those could churn, then the company would stand to lose 2.8 customers per month or 6.7% of its total customer base per year. In order for the company to maintain sales, it would need to win 2.8 new customers per month.

Marketing must deliver an additional 6.7% or 33.3 new customers per year just to stay even. With these numbers, we can now determine the level of sales and marketing required every month to achieve the corporate sales plan and win the 33 new customers to maintain even revenue and 133 new customers to grow revenue by 10% with the above assumptions.

Variations and complexity (not shown here) can be added, by using actual month-by-month customer contract renewal rates and actual churn rates to provide a more seasonal picture of the number of new customers required every month.

We can now also start asking "what if" questions. If the costs in customer acquisition across both selling and marketing are $3,000,000 and the investment in churn mitigation marketing is $250,000, then we can now start to determine whether an investment in churn mitigation is more valuable than the same investment in customer acquisition.

Value of Churn Mitigation Marketing

Let's assume that the $100,000 in churn mitigation marketing (and selling) has been determined to reduce the churn rate by 10 points (from 20% down to 10%). That is, without this investment, the churn rate would have been 10% per month for contract-renewing customers. The lost customers per month would then be 1.39 versus 2.78 as shown in the spreadsheet below. This has a revenue implication of about $499,000 or a ROMI rate of 5.0. To keep the calculation simple, our calculation assumes the 3-year value of the newly won customer over 36 months. It doesn't include residual value of the customer in the 4th and out years, which is definitely not zero. Nor does the calculation include the potential future churn mitigation probability of this customer. That is, after 36 months, there is some non-zero probability that they will churn. We are also comparing only revenue to revenue. If the profits per customer were significantly different for new customers versus existing customers, then we would need to use an mROMI factor, which compares incremental profit per dollar in sales and marketing invested as opposed to incremental revenue per dollar invested.

Churn Analysis	
Marketing investment	$100,000
Average churn rate at 19%	1.39
Average churn rate at 20%	2.78
Revenue diff of churned customers (36 mo.)	$499,000
ROMI Rate (Churn Mitigation)	5.0

WITH GROWTH	Jan	Feb	Mar		Oct	Nov	Dec	Totals/ Averages
Baseline no new customers	500.0	500.0	500.0	...	500.0	500.0	500.0	500.0
Baseline revenue	$5,000,000	$5,000,000	$5,000,000	...	$5,000,000	$5,000,000	$5,000,000	$60,000,000
New customers	7.6	7.6	7.6	...	7.6	7.6	7.6	91.7
Total customers	507.6	515.3	522.9	...	576.4	584.0	591.7	549.65
Revenue with growth	$5,076,389	$5,152,778	$5,229,167	...	$5,763,889	$5,840,278	$5,916,667	$65,958,333
Revenue from all new customers (36 mo.)	$2,750,000	$2,750,000	$2,750,000	...	$2,750,000	$2,750,000	$2,750,000	$33,000,000

The case study above along with the illustrated business questions indicate the value of knowing the ROMI factors and how these can be used to build a marketing machine. In this case the ROMI Rate for Churn is 5.0 whereas for Customer Acquisition it is 22.0. Because we now know exactly what level of marketing and selling investments is required to perform these two functions, we can now also predict how much selling and marketing investment is required to achieve a 10% revenue growth, given our current contract mix and expected churn rate. Based on this simple example, the $100,000 currently invested in churn mitigation marketing could deliver significantly more revenue by reallocating it to customer acquisition. Specifically, it can deliver an incremental $1,700,000 ((22.0 – 5.0) * $100,000) due to the differences in ROMI rates (from 5.0 to 22.0).

Acquisition Marketing Analysis	
Marketing investment	$1,500,000
36 months revenue from new customers	$33,000,000
ROMI Rate (Customer Acquisition)	22.0

This is a simple application of objectives-based budgeting and the use of ROMI factors. There are a number of assumptions in this example; in particular, that the incremental revenue from an incremental investment in sales and marketing is linear. Typically, there would be diminishing returns for churn mitigation marketing and for customer acquisition marketing. It would be necessary to calculate these effects in order to determine the optimal mix between churn mitigation and customer acquisition.

A similar exercise can be done to determine the level of upselling and cross-selling required to increase revenue from existing customers, and whether investment in that is better or worse than an investment in customer acquisition. This is shown in the following supplemental case study for the telecommunications company example from above.

UPSELLING & CROSS-SELLING	Jan	Feb	Mar		Oct	Nov	Dec	Totals/ Averages
Baseline no new customers	500.0	500.0	500.0	...	500.0	500.0	500.0	500.0
Baseline revenue (No upselling)	$5,000,000	$5,000,000	$5,000,000	...	$5,000,000	$5,000,000	$5,000,000	$60,000,000
Upsold customers	25.0	25.0	25.0	...	25.0	25.0	25.0	300.0
Upsell revenue	$312,500	$312,500	$312,500	...	$312,500	$312,500	$312,500	$312,500
Customer revenue w/o upsell	$4,750,000	$4,500,000	$4,250,000	...	$2,500,000	$2,250,000	$2,000,000	
Total revenue with upsell	$5,062,500	$5,125,000	$5,187,500	...	$5,625,000	$5,687,500	$5,750,000	$64,875,000

Key Assumptions	
Average monthly revenue	$10,000
Upsell success rate	7.5%
Upsell revenue rate	25%

With this plan for upsell/cross-sell selling and marketing in place, the incremental revenue for the 36-month upsold contracts is $3.4m, with a ROMI rate for this function of 27.0. It is slightly more valuable than investing in new customer acquisition (ROMI rate of 22.0). The table below shows this impact:

UPSELLING & CROSS-SELLING ANALYSIS	
Marketing investment	$125,000
36 months revenue from upsold customers	$3,375,000
ROMI Rate (Customer Acquisition)	27.0

To complete the analysis, let's finally assume that analytics isn't cost-free. Assuming we invest $75,000 per year in analytics and are able to increase the upselling success from 7% over three years to 9%, then the ROMI on analytics is 9 (see table below).

IMPOVED UPSELLING ANALYTICS ANALYSIS	
Revenue at 7.5%	$3,375,000
Revenue at 9.0%	$4,050,000
Difference	$675,000
Incremental analytics investment	$75,000
ROMI rate of incremental analytics investment	9.0

This case study illustrates the primary types of marketing as they relate to one-on-one customer relationships. It requires that we separate our marketing budgets into categories related specifically to the following clear-cut objectives:

1. **New customer acquisition** – New customer acquisition marketing includes activities such as awareness generation, customer nurturing, lead qualification marketing, proposal generation, and retargeting. These can be executed through mass media, trade show marketing, inbound marketing, and many other types of marketing activities. Each of these activities could be made up of specific media channels with very specific new customer acquisition messages.

2. **Existing customer marketing and selling account support** – Existing customer marketing and selling account support should typically be factored into the marketing budget to some extent. Existing customers need some ongoing communications from the marketing team and the sales team in order to maintain their satisfaction levels, as well as their desire to renew their contracts. There is typically some fixed cost involved, but it could be as simple as a quarterly visit from the salesperson, a bi-monthly call from an inside account executive, or a subscription to a corporate newsletter to check in on their current status and to see if there are any open issues that need to be remedied.

3. **Upselling and cross-selling** – For B2B marketers, upselling and cross-selling can often be undertaken either by an internal sales team or an outside account executive to further understand customer needs and monitor those needs as they change over time.

171

For consumer marketers, new services can be packaged and made available—for example, new data plans for mobile users or new cable packages for cable users—to entice customers to upgrade their service plans. These can be promoted through an outbound telemarketing campaign, direct (snail) mail, email, or mass media. For B2B marketers, upselling can promote new software features or new product capabilities as they are made available.

4. **Win-back marketing** – Customers that have terminated their relationship with the company can sometimes be won back through marketing. It could be that they have buyer's remorse with the new company, or the competitive offer wasn't as good as originally perceived—any number of reasons that could be hypothesized and applied to win them back. Marketing activities in this category typically comprise direct marketing through snail mail, email, or outbound telemarketing.

5. **Rescue marketing** – If a customer declares their desire to cancel their contract, but hasn't yet canceled or is in the process of cancelling, the sales team, customer service, or marketing in general can try to rescue these accounts through special offers or directing them to speak with a sales supervisor, who may have more leeway in providing an offer to keep them on as a customer. It is critical to set aside a budget for these types of offers, but not make them widely known, since savvy customers may try and game the system every time their contracts are up for renewal.

6. **Advocacy marketing** – Advocacy marketing can be done in a number of ways. For B2B marketers this could be done via user groups, online support forums, and many other online social media platforms. In the consumer space, this can be encouraged through online contests or sweepstakes for positive review submissions in social media.

7. **Brand-Building** – Lastly, there are certain marketing activities that can't be directly tied to one of the above objectives, but are certainly valuable in their ability to increase the effectiveness of marketing materials and drive value across all the above categories. To drive value, a first-level simplification could be to allocate the brand-building investment proportionately across each of the

other six categories to attribute the value of brand-building to the marketing mix.

Marketing activities for any of the above categories can be easily identified and disaggregated to point to specific objectives for the marketing budgeting process. This provides a very instructive and valuable communications tool for the rest of the company to start to understand how marketing and selling activities can be targeted to meet corporate objectives as they relate to the phases of the customer relationship.

Objectives-based budgeting by product (or service)

New product launch and cannibalization

Marketing also needs to target its marketing budgets based on product status. Just about every company has existing products or services that fit in any one of the following categories: new features, new products, seasonal variants, channel-specific variants, and products to be discontinued. In any given year, revenue is being generated by each of these product types and marketing (and selling) activities are taking place to support each of these states. Failing to allocate marketing investments across each of these states can lead to imbalances in the marketing mix and lost revenue opportunities for the company (see case study).

Case study: Consumer packaged goods, new product launch, and cannibalization

A consumer packaged goods company determined that an innovation in the hand and body lotion category could grow the category and deliver new functionality not previously available. Through detailed consumer research, the company determined that hand and body lotion with a self-tanning function could provide additional benefits throughout the year for women looking to improve their overall skin tone. Because many women use lotion to moisturize and soften their skin, this self-tanning capability could provide a new benefit that could become a major differentiator.

Case study: Consumer packaged goods, new product launch, and cannibalization (cont'd)

Prior to the launch, tanning lotions were always sold as a separate product and generally sold only in the Summer months. They were sold as "self-tanners" and not considered as part of the hand and body lotion category. By adding small amounts of the tanning compounds to traditional lotions, women would be able to soften their skin while also adding color. Because the lotion contained only small amounts of the self-tanning function, through daily use it was easy to generate a great looking color without streaking.

The new self-tanning product was launched by one of the major competitors in the category and was very successful, moving to being one of the leading brands in the category. It was launched with a strong marketing campaign, however, the marketing budget normally designated for the existing products was cannibalized in order for the overall brand spending to stay within their top-line expense budget. Because of this the launch was successful, but the existing non-self-tanning variants suffered significantly. The net revenue across both sets was then significantly less than had the brand maintained the marketing position of the existing variants and had allocated a separate incremental budget for the support of the new, self-tanning variants.

The situation discussed in the case study above is very typical for many companies. Often, sales for the new product are expected to be great without any expected decrease in the sales volumes of the existing products. To remedy this oversight, the company must endeavor to properly allocate marketing funds for the new product launch without necessarily cannibalizing the marketing budget for existing products. Or, the sales for the existing products must be expected to decline with the lack of marketing support. In almost all cases, the sales of the existing products suffer. If applied properly, the marketing machine can determine the level of interaction and the cannibalization of the sales of existing products. In this way, the impact of the reduced allocation of marketing support can be known ahead of time so that volume expectations can be properly set.

With this information two things can happen: either the optimal mix of marketing can be determined for the new and the existing brands from the total marketing budget; or additional funds can be justified to fully support the launch of the new brand without the unintended consequences of strong losses with the existing brand.

Product variants

Launching product variants can be done to increase the overall category size for the long term, provide seasonal variation to meet seasonal requirements, or simply to bring engagement back to the core product variant.

Often strong brands offer new flavor variants to their existing popular products. In the fall, Starbucks offers a pumpkin-spice flavored coffee. For Christmas, Oreo offers green and red colored fillings. Stolichnaya offers Salted Karamel flavored vodka. These have many interesting effects as they relate to product-based budgeting.

For Starbucks and Oreo, these are seasonal variants that provide added lift during the season. In some cases, the sales of the seasonal variants detract from the base variant. In others, they bring consumers back to the brand and increase overall sales. The promotions around the new variant may simply be done to increase overall sales of the base variant. Or the sales of the new variant are so strong that the flavor can stand on its own and become a permanent member of the offered variants. For example, Stolichnaya Salted Karamel could fall into this category if it survives on the shelf for more than just a few months.

This means that each of these product variants requires a different marketing budget depending on whether the objective is for it to be offered as a seasonal variant, a base variant builder, or a potential new permanent offering.

Product states

The marketing budget needs to be allocated according to each of these product states. These marketing allocations can be delineated as follows:

1. **Existing base variant marketing** – Existing products continue to need to be promoted—this is the majority of activities in this category.
2. **Add-on features** – Activations promoting add-on features can be done separately from promotions for the base product or they can be done in conjunction with them, depending on whether the objective is to sell more base products with the new feature, or whether the new feature is to be sold completely separately. In the latter case, the

based product with the new feature is closer to being considered a separate new product. For example, ads for the foot-activated lift on a Ford Escape falls into this category.

3. **New product introductions** – New product introductions can either stand on their own or bring excitement back to the base variant. Because new products often distract the company and the marketing team from the base variant, the marketing for a new product introduction must be carefully scrutinized. The objectives need to be clearly defined so that the marketing budgets can be appropriately allocated and sales of the existing variant don't suffer greatly while the new variant is being introduced. New product introductions can also include new packaging of an existing product, although these generally fall into the add-on feature category unless the new package includes a significantly valuable new feature. For example, a pump bottle feature could fall into this category.

4. **Seasonal product variant introductions** – Seasonal variants can often grow the category during the chosen season and also bring consumers back to the base brand. The Starbucks pumpkin-spice flavored coffee falls into this category.

5. **Experimental product introductions** – In some cases, marketers introduce new variants to test whether there is truly a need for them. This is often the case with online marketing, where the testing can be done quite easily and new variants can be offered for a short time and then quickly removed from the market after their success provides the desired insights into the market.

6. **Channel-specific variants** – In some markets, channel-specific variants can be developed for large channel partners, or they can be offered in such a way that nearly identical offerings can be made. For example, consumer electronics retailers wish to claim to have the lowest prices on a manufacturer's products. This is achieved by offering two slightly different variants: one for each retailer, such that, each variant being offered by the retailer truly does have the lowest price in the market.

7. **Product discontinuation** – An additional product state related to marketing is product discontinuation. When a product is to be discontinued, it sometimes needs to be removed from inventory

and the store shelves in order to make room for the new replacement product. Sometimes this includes the manufacturer taking back unsold inventory or selling it on promotion. Typically, in the fall in the automotive industry, for example, when the new models become available, summer-end promotions are done to clear the inventory of the old models to make room for the new line when it is introduced.

It is critical to understand each of these and other dimensions of product marketing in order to appropriately allocate funds so that an optimal mix of marketing activities can be planned in the product state dimension.

Objectives-based budgeting by channel

Marketing activities can also be allocated based on the channel activities driving the business. Marketers can allocate their channel funds into several areas:

1. **Promotions with existing partners** – Marketers must continue to support their current channel partners to help them push the products through to the consumer. This can take place in many forms, but is often configured as a BOGO (Buy One Get One free) or some other temporary price reduction to allow the channel to sell the same volume at higher margins, or to sell more volume at a reduced price and margin. In many cases, these can be funded through co-op programs with the distribution partner.
2. **Promotions to win new channel partners** – Especially with small brands in large markets, marketers often work to build new distribution channels. Marketing investments to sign up these partners and promote the channel to the consumer would be allocated here.
3. **Promotions to discontinue channel partners** – Typically marketing funds are not necessary to discontinue a channel partnership, unless the partner has significant inventory that needs to be flushed through to the consumer to close out the relationship without the need for manufacturer buybacks.

Objectives-based budgeting by price/promotion

The last dimension important for disaggregating the marketing budget has to do with price. Products can be sold with different prices when there is a national border to be crossed or just to offer certain prices to certain customer sets. Volume discounts and other price offers can be made as long as they follow specific government guidelines. However, prices can easily vary when sold with coupons or BOGOs, or back-to-school specials or other promotions. These customer promotions are often funded directly or indirectly out of the marketing budget.

Quite often, there isn't a specific budget for price offers. However, if this is a major part of the marketing mix, then they need to be tracked and managed. Because price offers decrease the overall margin, they need to be accounted for and someone needs to be responsible for them. Some companies do have specific budgets set aside for this non-revenue item so that marketers or the sales team can be held responsible for the overall level of discounts given. Generally, there are only a few top-level types of price offers, although, depending on the business, the product volume sold on discount can be disaggregated further to fit the needs of the reporting structure. Here are three typical types of price variations:

1. **Product volume sold at full price** – This is typically the full manufacturer's suggested retail price (MSRP).
2. **Product volume sold on discount to the channel** – The marketing machine needs to track channel promotions, such as volume bonuses offered to the channel and not necessarily flowed through to the consumer. These trade promotions include actions, such as a case free for every ten cases purchased.
3. **Product volume sold on discount to the consumer** – The marketing machine needs to track the discounts sold at the consumer level with a rebate, coupon, or a BOGO without necessarily the option for the channel to participate. These offers can sometimes be made where the channel can also participate at some level without losing their profit margins.

Summary of objectives-based budgeting

The above discussion helps marketers build a marketing budget disaggregated along the customer dimension as well as 3 dimensions of the 4Ps: product, place, and price. Many times, these actions can work in combination. In order to build the marketing machine, each of the single or combined effects needs to be accounted for, measured, and budgeted such that the company can better track, manage, and optimize the investments fed into the marketing machine.

Lastly, the promotion P is one that can apply to some or all of the 3 dimensions discussed above. If we picture the 4 dimensions above (customer, product, channel and price) as making up a grid of many small 1x1x1x1 cells, then marketing (media and sales) actions can be applied to each cell separately or across multiple cells in order to build a media budget, a sales budget, manage the media investments, and build a marketing machine that is predictable and accountable across the entire marketing spectrum. For example, brand advertising would apply to all cells, although maybe not equally across all cells.

Depending on the size of the organization, each group of cells needs to have a specific marketing manager assigned. If the organization is large enough, each cell requires a separate manager. These cells must report up in such a way that there is a pre-eminent focus on the consumer and the segment.

The top-level manager is responsible for developing the plan for each cell and is responsible for the achievement within each cell, as well as tracking and integrating any new competitive or consumer trends.

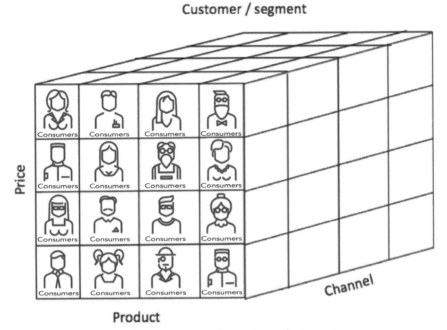

Figure 9: Objectives-based marketing budgeting matrix

Data, automation, analytics, regulations and artificial intelligence

Marketing is moving rapidly toward a high level of technology and automation. Larger marketing teams have begun hiring for a Marketing IT position in order to develop a marketing IT strategy and manage its roll-out. There are tens of thousands of new applications, data sets, automations, and analytic methods already available, and many more are being introduced every day. Each has its own capabilities, advantages, and target areas in the marketing value chain.

Data

Almost daily, new third-party data sets are being made available to the marketplace. Many data sets are spin-offs of other applications with additional marketing value in tracking and providing deep insight into consumer behavior. New, real-time data sets help campaigns provide additional value in targeting consumer groups at the right time, right place with the right creative to increase engagement and conversion.

Data quality is one of the chief concerns of an analytics system. Marketing data specialists must develop methods to handle the many potential errors in the data. Checking for inconsistencies, missing data, outliers, double entries, and other anomalies is a continuous challenge, and much resource needs to be applied to this function. The process of data cleansing is iterative and ongoing.

The goal of the data is threefold: First, it is used to improve the buying, placing and creation of an ad. Second, it is used to improve response measurement so marketers can track, measure and optimize success. Third, it is used to diagnose problems that may arise. Each of these methods can provide significant value in improving overall marketing success and ROI.

In an ideal world, data would be continuously, accurately, and instantaneously available down to the level of detail of an individual consumer. Unfortunately, it is often available weeks later at some level of aggregation with missing data and doesn't align easily with other data sources. The timing of this data, whether it's available on a daily, weekly, monthly or quarterly cycle, will define the marketing machine workflow in terms of what activities can be done in each week and day of the rolling planning process.

Automation (and programmatic ad buying)

With the enormous volume of data becoming part of the online advertising eco-system, automation is the only way to take advantage of the value they can provide. Many previously manual functions are now being replaced by automation and programmatic interfaces. The advancement of automation will continue as digital advertising progresses and new opportunities to provide increased value to the marketing value chain become known. Industry standards will govern how applications work and communicate together to build and grow this online advertising ecosystem.

Analytics

New analytic methods are now becoming available to make use of these vast volumes of data. Big Data by its sheer size impacts the ability of computing resources to analyze data in a reasonable amount of time. Statistical methods may be applied, but may not be able to be run in a reasonable amount of time to present an ad before the consumer gets frustrated or loses patience. New analytics methods may be required. Even excluding communications delays, real-time analytics requires the calculation and result to be concluded within 100 to 200 milliseconds. With non-real-time analytics, analysts are willing to wait a few seconds or perhaps a few hours, but no one finds it acceptable to wait a few weeks. With these vast amounts of data, new analytic methods are being developed to provide near-accurate solutions in a much shorter time, as opposed to 100% accurate solutions in a much longer timeframe. With these significant time savings, new business opportunities can become a reality. When advanced analytics can increase sales conversions by .1% on a $10bn+ revenue brand, it translates into an increase of tens of millions. Marketers must now look for these new methods and build them into their marketing machine in order to build intellectual property and protectable competitive advantage.

With data accuracy never at 100%, algorithms must be able to work with imperfect data and yet still provide reasonably accurate results and recommendations. In addition, algorithms need to be written to potentially fill in and correct missing or potentially/confirmed erroneous data.

Regulations

The FCC in the U.S. and the European Commission in the EU are starting to catch up to complaints by consumers about how their personal data is being captured, stored, and used. The recent release of the new General Data Protection Regulation (GDPR) in the European Union is a sign of things to come. Many more countries and regions will follow suit with ever stricter regulations. These regulations are intended to help reduce the risks of personal private data use by advertisers. It is intended to reduce the loss of privacy associated with data breaches, and to reduce the level of data that can be collected by the advertiser. Marketing IT and legal will need to carefully track and weigh the impact of each of the new regulations as they go into force.

Artificial intelligence

Artificial intelligence represents the next wave of analytic methods to provide fast, affordable, and reliable analytics of massive data sets. IBM's Watson is already making inroads, both on the analytics side and on the creative side. Artificial intelligence can be likened to automating the analytic process, generating many new insights out of new and existing data sets. On the creative side, ads are being developed that can interactively communicate with the consumer in real time. For example, augmented reality and virtual reality are beginning to make inroads into the retail shopping experience to provide additional realism to product demos. Interactive displays providing interactive communication back to the viewer are making inroads into the mall shopping experience. Each of these and many more examples may transform the future of the brick-and-mortar shopping experience that marketers can take advantage of.

Chapter 12

Final Considerations for a Marketing Machine

Media strategy in the midst of mass media and individualized media

Media has two dimensions: mass media (where advertisers target some broad reach of specific groups of individuals) and individual media (where advertisers target a specific individual, even though we may not know exactly who that individual is).

Mass media

Mass media is often thought of as traditional media. Advertisers insert television commercials and they are placed on programs watched primarily by a specific demographic, e.g., women aged 25 to 39 or men aged 40 to 59. Or these groups can be targeted through a sports sponsorship, which could be signage at a baseball game or the naming rights to a stadium. Typically, the impressions are very inexpensive compared to other media. Mass media channels include PR, sponsorships, some search ads, TV, radio, print, billboards, some digital display ads, some social display ads, and many others.

With mass media, there is a probability that a specific individual will see the ad and respond to it, but the individual is not directly targeted.

Figure 10: AT&T Stadium

Individualized media

With individualized media, the advertiser is trying to reach a specific individual, not a specific group of unknown individuals. A specific individual is known, and certain criteria about that individual are also known. Typical individualized marketing can include direct mail pieces, CRM contacts, retargeting, email lists, and outbound telemarketing lists. Individualized media is where many new marketing opportunities are found. New types of lists can be purchased or generated with great detail on how these individuals have behaved in the past, along with some level of demographic or firmographic data. With this data, very specific messages can be delivered with high expectations of a response.

These lists can identify individuals with a specific credit-worthiness, past click behavior, past purchase behavior, and many important attributes that help to improve the odds of their response and decrease the cost of their conversion to a customer or repeat customer. These lists also allow a series of messages to be delivered to the individual, so that they can be sequenced or simply repeated until a desired response takes place.

For the CEO

Retargeting is the marketer's new best friend. Once an individual has visited a website, a cookie can be placed on their browser or their mobile ID can be identified. Then they can be provided follow-up messages *after* they leave the website.

In this way, as individuals work their way down the purchase funnel, they can continue to receive messages from the brand until some point in the future. In this way, the brand can more easily stay top of mind as that individual traverses the funnel. The individual is targeted with an ad on other sites as they browse the web. Depending on the category, typically 30 to 40 retargeted impressions may be required before that individual finally converts.

The value of data in the marketing machine

Data is everywhere, but it ages quickly. The average relocation rate in the U.S. is 11%.[42] This means that geographic data, if not updated, will be only 89% accurate after one year and 79% accurate after 2 years. This means that roughly one out of every five consumers' geographic data will be incorrect. In the U.S., for B2B companies, the average length of time a worker stays with the same company is 4.4 years.[43] This means that every year about 23%[44] of the customer database will change. For millennials, the rate is even higher. All of this matters because data accuracy is critical to marketing effectiveness, loyalty, and a brand's reputation.

There are many types of data. Some can be very valuable for some industries and less so for others. In consumer markets, life-stage, demographic, and psychographic data can be significant sources of marketing strategies and tactics. Below are a handful of challenges and opportunities related to all data sources. Generally, any data set imaginable is available with any level of completeness and accuracy. It is only limited by the cost the marketer is willing to invest.

---

[42] http://www.mymovingreviews.com/move/how-often-and-why-americans-move, from the US Census Bureau comparison of 2012 and 2013, Oct 2016

[43] http://www.forbes.com/sites/jeannemeister/2012/08/14/job-hopping-is-the-new-normal-for-millennials-three-ways-to-prevent-a-human-resource-nightmare/#7be757d15508, Bureau of Labor Statistics, Oct 2016

[44] The rate at which a B2B customer database changes is calculated by assuming that 1/4.4 (~23%) employees will change jobs every year.

Bad data and lowered marketing effectiveness

Bad/inaccurate data reduces the accuracy of databases, especially those based on look-alike models. Look-alike models tend to amplify the inaccuracies and therefore reduce the overall ROI. It is impossible to keep all customer data totally up to date. For most companies, correction of key customer data is manual, requiring time and money, but there are new systems coming online that use machine learning to automate the correction of many of these errors.

Customer loyalty

Best-in-class marketers have typically invested heavily in keeping their data accurate. Consumers no longer compare the quality of your service and loyalty with that of a brand's immediate peers. The brand's consumer and loyalty service quality is compared against best-in-class marketers, so bad data quality can lead to lowered loyalty and satisfaction ratings, as well as reduced levels of advocacy. Errors in consumer data, such as promoting women's products to male consumers or local promotions offered for consumers in one state reaching consumers living in another, can destroy the relationship with a brand.

Data from every touchpoint

Data can be captured or programmatically built into the web presentation at every touchpoint in the purchase process. If the data is captured incorrectly and that mistake leads to an erroneous presentation at some other touchpoint, this will reduce the accuracy of the message and generally lead to lower marketing ROI and effectiveness. It may also lead to a dissatisfying customer experience.

Operational data

In-store data, web behavior data, call-in data, and past purchase behavior data are valuable sources of data that can add to the accuracy of the marketing machine. With this information, top-level creative and media strategies can be developed and media tactics can be optimized.

Reputation management

With the advent of easy and ubiquitous social media, when brands make errors in the customer experience, it's very easy for a disgruntled consumer to post it in their online community. Negative advocacy is the new watchword for the challenges of delivering a high-quality customer experience. Keeping consumer data quality as accurate as possible is critical for reputation management and reduction in negative advocacy.

Social media data

Apart from being a venue to share brand opinions, social media has turned into an excellent source of highly accurate consumer demographic information. Because many social media platforms capture an individual's personal data, the individual tends to keep it up to date and make the actual corrections themselves. For example, the individual enters their birth date and the city where they live. If they move, they will tend to quickly update their city of residence. This means that the social media platform can maintain a relatively constant level of accuracy of their demographic data. Where it tends to become inaccurate depends on the specific social media platform. Here are a few examples:

LinkedIn

LinkedIn usage waxes and wanes with many people, depending on whether they are actively job-searching or not. Some individuals keep their profiles up to date, except for immediately after a job change, when there may be a lag of a month or so. Also, because it is such a good source of B2B employee data, senior executives have begun to abandon or close their profiles in order to avoid the onslaught of marketing sales spam that they attract through these platforms.

Facebook

Facebook profiles are generally kept up to date because they represent the persona of the individual, so the accuracy is very high. Mobile IDs (not numbers) and email addresses are generally accurate, and Facebook does a good job (although not perfect) of matching work and personal emails to an account. This is changing as Millennials graduate from college and are bombarded with advertising (and employers). They often close their pre-graduation accounts and open a new, sanitized job-seeker account to erase past posts. Some even cancel their accounts altogether due to the high volume of advertising targeting taking place upon graduation. Nevertheless, across the platform accounts are generally accurate and kept up to date. This means that using this data to leverage other consumer-level data can be very valuable.

Twitter

Because it is generally easier to set up an account on Twitter than on other platforms, and because multiple accounts can be set up by a single individual, these accounts are typically less accurate than Facebook.

Other external factors in social media

Temporary closures of ad networks due to accreditation issues can impact the ability of an advertiser to continue advertising with their best network with the best ROI. For example, on October 13, 2016, the Media Rating Council suspended accreditation of Google's DoubleClick for not adhering to the April 2016 mobile metrics guidelines.[45] If this were a major source of advertising for a brand, it could have led to short-term inaccuracies in their marketing machines.

Event-triggered advertising

New opportunities are being developed that allow real-time advertising triggered by specific events. Marketers can advertise to an individual based on their geo-location, or they can advertise based on the actual weather conditions found at a particular moment in time. As these new sources of advertising become available, marketers will be able to increase their effectiveness further and provide improved marketing effectiveness.

---

[45] http://www.mediapost.com/publications/article/286807/google-to-regain-mrc-accreditation-for-doubleclick.html?utm_source=newsletter&utm_medium=email&utm_content=headline&utm_campaign=97269, October 2016.

Using consumer-level data to drive marketing effectiveness

Gathering accurate and timely consumer-level data, and understanding its implications, is paramount to building a successful marketing machine. It not only allows for optimization of consumer-centric communications but also for a better understanding of the market and the ability to react faster, especially with digital media.

Consumer-level data comes from many sources; for the data to be aggregated across these sources, it needs to be matched between the sources with a valid key.

Problems with data matching

Let's assume that Sally Pierson lived at 301 North Elm Street in Chicago when she signed up for a J.Crew loyalty card. She visited the J.Crew website with her desktop, tablet, and phone. Because she is a member of the loyalty program, each of these devices is tied back to her in a deterministic way. In 2014, she moves to New York and now lives at 2401 13th St in Manhattan, but her phone number hasn't changed and she continues to shop at J.Crew in New York and elsewhere. Sally never updated her mailing address in the J.Crew CRM system. Because of this erroneous data it would be a waste of advertising to send Sally promotional info on new jeans at the Chicago store, when she now lives and only shops for jeans in New York.

In order to correct this error, the J.Crew website needs to detect that all devices now access the loyalty program from a New York location. Once this is detected, the website needs to send a notification for Sally to update her home address. In this way J.Crew would be able to reduce the number of location errors in the database and improve overall direct marketing effectiveness.

There are two primary consumer-level data matching methods.

Deterministic matching

Deterministic matching is explicitly related to a single individual. If a consumer visits a website on their mobile device, deterministic matching would match their desktop, smart television, game console, and tablet specifically back to that individual based on some type of matching algorithm.

Deterministic matching and online behavior

Online behavior is deterministic, but instead of being matched to an individual, it is tied to his or her browser. Online behavior and data can be captured through a form or web click behavior and connected to their IP address. A cookie can be placed on their desktop browser identifying that browser for future advertising. If Jim viewed a golf accessories page for 2 minutes and then read news about his favorite baseball team, it would be ideal, when he visits an advertising-enabled site on the same device, to present him with an ad with either golf- or baseball-themed messages to improve his likelihood to eventually respond. Knowing this past click behavior can lead to significantly better targeting and ad placement, as well as improved creative concept presentation, but getting the match wrong can easily lead to less than stellar results. This is the value of matching behavior deterministically and then choosing the right media action (message, channel, creative, and frequency) to capitalize on that knowledge.

Furthermore, when Jim switches to another device, such as his mobile or laptop, it would be ideal to present the right golf or baseball ad to him again in order to continue the brand building that started on his desktop. This is especially true now that 60% of internet activity takes place on mobile devices. However, there are technical challenges in mobile matching. In mobile there are no cookies, and the cookie from the desktop browser is of no value when the individual is on their mobile unless there is a way to match that mobile phone back to the desktop browser and cookie. Google and other advertising platforms have begun to solve this challenge and are beginning to provide good matching across user devices.

Instead, in mobile research marketers, look at Apple or Android (or other) device IDs. The identification of the individual now needs to take place through this ID, and this ID needs to be matched back to the desktop browser cookie in the above example. To maximize effectiveness, marketers, advertisers, agencies, and adtech providers are striving to find ways to accurately match individuals to multiple devices, so that ads can be presented, accurately and timely, to the same individual, whether on mobile, tablet, desktop, smart television, or game console.

Lastly, deterministic matching can also be foiled by typos in a matching data field or address changes, as in the J.Crew example above. They can also be foiled by simply using different methods to enter the same name. In most cases, IBM is the same as Ibm Corporation. It is also the same as IBM corporation. But within an algorithmic, deterministic matching method, these company names may not be properly identified and matched 100% of the time.

Probabilistic matching

Probabilistic matching uses a statistical approach to match data from two separate data sets. Data can be captured for a group of individuals, as in through a segmentation study. If an individual belongs to a particular segment, then certain preferences and attitudes are assigned to that individual. If 30% of the segment are defined as male, then without further information, 30% of the individuals are assigned as male based on probabilistic matching.

Data can also be matched in a probabilistic way using look-alike modeling. Look-alike modeling assigns a trait to an individual because they have similar traits and characteristics to others in a segment or database.

Geo-Matching

There are other methods becoming available that are adding to the matching accuracy and value. Geo-matching tracks the location of all devices, whether mobile or desktop, and uses that information to determine likely work locations and home locations. Family groups can be identified and even matched to smart TVs and other in-home devices.

In an ideal world, the marketer wants a single view of the consumer. Marketers don't want simply data; they want a consumer-level view. They don't want to have one view from a consumer's social media and a separate view from their digital presence. These views need to be matched with accuracy in order to maximize effectiveness and minimize wastage. As for the marketing machine, inaccuracies lead to less efficient marketing. Impressions are wasted on the wrong individuals. Messages aren't appropriate for the browser that receives the message. If the data accuracy varies wildly between media activities, this inaccuracy can have an impact on the ability of the marketing machine to be repeatable and predictive. Striving toward a single and accurate view of the consumer can significantly improve the effectiveness of the media. If its accuracy can be consistently improved, the effectiveness of the marketing machine will also improve.

Other issues with consumer data are below:

Deduping

When matching data sets, as shown with the IBM example above, addresses and names need to be deduped and cross-matched for best results.

Incomplete data

Very few data sources are complete. In an ideal world, a purchased data source would cover 100% of the target audience. But, unfortunately, this is never the case. Some data may cover 10%. Others may cover 65%. Each data source can offer significant value in improving marketing effectiveness for the consumers it covers, but it offers more if it is able to cover and align with other data sets. If the 10% coverage has 100% overlap with the 65%, then the 10% can be very valuable. If there is no overlap, then it may have less value. If there is partial overlap, but not in a deterministic way, that can pose different challenges as to how best to utilize the data sets.

Errors in the data

Very few data sets are 100% error-free. Even consumers can enter their own demographic data with errors. These errors may be accidental or on purpose. For many reasons, an individual may not want to provide certain private data for fear of loss of privacy or fear of cyber-crime on the data.

Detailed and accurate consumer-level data are critical not only to developing great media creative, placement, and buying, but also to gathering deep consumer insights and building effective marketing strategies. Competitive insights can also be gained, depending on the depth of the data, to the extent where consumers purchasing from or even just visiting a competitor can be detected and acted upon.

Data hierarchy

Lastly, there is a hierarchy in data. All data is not related directly to the individual; more often than not it is aggregated at some other level. It could be at the household level, at the shopper level, at the geographic level, or at the segment level. Matching each of these aggregated data sets to an individual is where challenges and errors can arise, making the marketing value of each new data set less than optimal.

Building an effective marketing machine with detailed individual consumer-level data can lead to significantly better marketing activities and overall effectiveness. Marketers must strive to research and identify new data sources that can provide added benefits in order to generate a payoff through improved marketing effectiveness.

Data errors

Birth date is the one piece of demographic information about an individual that can never change. A person's address, phone number, gender, email address—all are subject to change. It is these types of changes that cause errors in the assignment of specific matches to an individual. If the data sets aren't kept up to date, then marketing effectiveness suffers.

Media strategy and media buying

There are two phases to the optimization of the media budget. Optimization is important because, as marketers, we want to understand how we can achieve the highest level of conversion for the least cost. First, marketers must build a media strategy encompassing both mass media and individualized media. With the media strategy in place, marketers can then begin to buy media. Buying media has many unforeseeable influences. Sometimes they are known in advance, sometimes not.

Uncertain media costs

There are many influences driving the cost of media. These are determined by our actions, those of the competition, and those of the market at large. For example, advertising on television for a local New Jersey brand in the Philadelphia-New York corridor is often prohibitively expensive, since the complete audience of the New York DMA[46] needs to be purchased when only the New Jersey local audience is desired. The local target audience (at least without addressable TV) simply can't be purchased. Only the wider,

---

[46] DMA = Designated Market Area as defined by the Nielsen Company.

gross audience can be purchased. On the other hand, small advertisers can easily advertise in Charlotte, N.C., because when they do, the advertising only reaches that audience. The advertiser is paying for what they want to achieve; the gross market is the same as the target market.

Similarly, the cost of advertising in search and other digital properties is often determined by many market factors. If a business software brand had the name "Black Jack" and the marketer wanted to purchase search ad words including their brand name, the costs would be significantly higher because black jack is a term purchased frequently in the very competitive gambling market. Those marketers have a different ROI structure such that they can pay very high premiums for these search phrases.

Ad costs also vary over time and are to some extent dependent on the level of competitiveness at that moment for that particular online asset. If there are seasonalities in the market, in some months, keywords purchased in Google or Bing will be relatively inexpensive; in others, relatively expensive. This is the case in the furnace replacement market, because furnaces are searched for in the spring and fall months more so than in other months. Because of the seasonality in consumer purchase behavior for replacement furnaces, the prices for the furnace search term are much higher during the spring and fall and less expensive in the other months.

Costs on a daily basis may be unknown ahead of time, so advertisers must have the flexibility to purchase across several media channels to optimize their media buys. Some advertisers wait until the last few days of the month; prices are lower because their competitors have spent their budget in the beginning of the month.

The upfronts

Large media buys are influenced by the upfronts, which take place in the spring. Media owners contract to sell their upcoming fall advertising slots to prospective advertisers. Advertisers contract for a certain level of media investment and negotiate for the best terms for the audiences they wish to reach. The exact costs aren't known ahead of time, so the level of media purchased may vary between the media strategy and the media buy. Also, deals can be made where if certain audience levels aren't achieved by the media owner, make-goods are given to provide compensation for unachieved viewership by the media owner or the network.

Other effects may also impact the level of success of the media, such as position in the commercial pod, not allowing other competing brands to advertise directly prior to or after your placement, and so on.

Adblocking

Many individuals are retaliating against the onslaught of digital advertising by installing ad-blocking software. This software is designed to block all ads from appearing in the individual's browsers. The media owner, or publisher, is mostly harmed in that the content is provided to the individual, but the publisher isn't compensated by the advertiser since the ad wasn't presented when the content was delivered.

Advertisers are also harmed by adblocking, but to a lesser extent. If the individual belongs to a desired audience, then the advertiser can't deliver messages to that individual except through other means. Because the most prevalent users of ad blockers are in the most valuable audience (Millennials), it's becoming more and more difficult for advertisers to reach their target audiences at reasonable cost.

Viewability

Advertisers purchase media so that it will be viewed by the target audience and target individual. In many cases, the ad isn't viewable and therefore isn't seen by the target. It may be below-the-fold, covered by another window, or not on the screen long enough to be visually registered. The advertising industry is currently setting standards for viewability depending on the type of ad, but even these standards are in flux and may continue to be in flux for another few years. This means that even though we may have purchased a million impressions in a particular media channel, we may not have actually presented a million *viewable* impressions at the same quality level that we planned for.

There are other issues impacting the execution of the media strategy during the media-buying process. What this means for the marketing machine is that marketers must constantly review their level of success in order to deliver on their promise of a certain level of sales for a certain level of investment.

It also means that advertisers need to build the marketing machine both top down and bottom up. They need to start strategically, but also realize that there are nuances in each media channel to take into consideration in order to build a complete and solid media strategy; the media strategy is just one leg of any go-to-market strategy made up of the popular 4Ps[47]—Product, Price, Place, and Promotion.

Data security and control

The marketing machine is the crown jewel of the company intellectual property. If it is hacked or key knowledge is lost or stolen, it could represent a major loss to the company. Not only does it bring in all relevant competitive and consumer data, which in itself is confidential and requires a high level of security, but the machine itself (how it is built, the rules and algorithms and intellectual prowess built into the machine, the team, and the processes surrounding the machine) includes critical elements of the company's trade secrets. These must be guarded with the highest levels of security.

In addition to the marketing machine, one of the most highly protected and regulated types of data that may be included within the marketing machine is PII (Personally Identifiable Information) data. It is often a critical component of many marketing machines. If this data is compromised, it can lead to significant losses in brand and company image, damaged consumer confidence, government fines, and consumer lawsuits.

Although the analytics itself often works with anonymized data, the proximity of this data to the marketing machine is also a liability that must be carefully considered.

Single consumer view

Central to the design of the marketing machine is to build a single consumer view. Siloes of data made up of social behavior, digital behavior, and third-party data need to be broken down so that this data can be fully integrated

---

[47] Kotler, Philip, Kevin L. Keller, Fabio Ancarani, and Michele Costabile. *Marketing management 14/e*. Pearson, 2014.

into a complete, 360-degree view of the consumer. The machine needs to house all primary and secondary research in appropriate ways so that it can be quickly applied to the analytics within the machine. The marketing machine must be the one complete view of this data that not only provides the ability to better purchase data, but also to build the critical decision methods to respond appropriately and timely to competitive actions and channel or external factors.

Production scaling

Unfortunately, especially for larger companies with large consumer bases, the volume of data and analytics that can be done at an individual consumer level is very high. This requires new techniques to scale up the analytics and algorithms or to aggregate the analyses where necessary. In some cases, the machine must respond at the individual level. In others, it may only need to respond at a segment level. Computational power needs to be easily scaled up when optimization routines are run, or scaled down during quiescent periods between analyses. In addition, the marketing machine may also require other aggregation and disaggregation methods to quickly analyze and develop answers to questions relating to potential future scenarios. The scaling of the machine must be determined to be able to respond at any appropriate level in a short period of time.

Chapter 13

Summary

Those companies without a marketing machine will be at a disadvantage in the marketplace. They will be up against competition that can be counted on to deliver revenue and volume at a consistent and predictable rate for a given investment. An effective marketing machine will provide value to shareholders because their risks will be lower—and investors will be more willing to invest in the company because of this reduced market risk. With the rise of digital marketing, the connection between marketing investment and response is tightly coupled, making it more possible and easier to build successful and accurate marketing machines.

A marketing machine not only impacts the company's fortunes, but has effects that resonate all throughout the company and the investor community. Marketing management turnover will be reduced because they will be better at delivering on expectations. Marketing staff will turn over less because marketing management will turn over less. The company's operations department will be able to streamline their activities because they will be able to produce a more predictable volume plan. The C-Suite will be better able to negotiate the vicissitudes of the corporate planning and budgeting process because there will be more certainty in the top line projections.

Through the use of a fully implemented marketing machine, the company will be able to reap more profit from its marketing investments because it will have a detailed and accurate understanding of marketing ROI and how results in the marketplace are directly connected to specific marketing actions and investments. Risks are minimized through constant tracking of pertinent competitive, channel, and external factors. Because achievement is highly certain, costs throughout the company can be better managed.

"If it were easy then we'd already be doing it."

Understanding and learning from the future is a critical element in the marketing machine. The marketing machine must take into consideration the immediate future all the way out to the distant future, so the company can best achieve the targets in front of it with the allocated budgets and investments.

A marketing machine can be implemented at various levels by every type of company. Each company may require different types of data, analytics, or processes, but the core components of a marketing machine are required for companies to survive and thrive in the short and long term.

Implementing a marketing machine is both easy and difficult. It is conceptually simple and the concept behind it is expected from the investments in every other part of the company. Why shouldn't the most important function in the company be held accountable for delivering on key objectives tied to achieving the annual corporate sales and profit targets?

On the other hand, implementing a marketing machine is difficult because of past history. Marketers in the past have been held accountable to spending to budget. Because marketing was seen as an expense, it was one of the first line items to be cut. With a marketing machine, marketing will finally be treated as an investment in future sales. A cut in marketing will directly lead to a cut in future sales. Changing this mindset both at the CEO level and within the marketing function will meet with a lot of resistance. The creative team will fear losing the freedom to come up with great ads that break through and build the brand. The rest of the marketing team will now realize that their mortgages are now tied to their actions. Formerly, task-oriented marketers will now need to change their mindsets from completing the given task on time and under budget to achieving the sales targets with the given budget.

The hardest part of implementing a marketing machine is simply taking the first step. So, just get started. Turn that cog. Pull that lever. Push that button.

THE END

Index